LOCAL SEO FOR RESTAURANTS

TIPS AND MARKETING STRATEGIES TO OPTIMIZE GOOGLE MY BUSINESS AND MASTER LOCAL MARKETING FOR GROWTH

RESTAURANT MARKETING BLUEPRINT
BOOK 4

JON NELSEN

DO SOCIAL SMARTER, LLC

marketing   est 2017

Local SEO for Restaurants: Tips and Marketing Strategies to Optimize Google My Business and Master Local Marketing for Growth

CONTENTS

INTRODUCTION

Turn casual diners into loyal fans with Do Social Smarter's proven system to grow your customer base, boost reviews, and drive foot traffic effortlessly.

Visit DoSocialSmarter.com today and discover how to keep your seats full and your competition behind.

DO SOCIAL SMARTER, LLC

marketing   est. 2017

CHAPTER 1
UNDERSTANDING LOCAL SEO FOR RESTAURANTS

WHY LOCAL SEO IS THE KEY TO DRIVING MORE CUSTOMERS THROUGH YOUR DOORS

A well-crafted local SEO strategy is like having a well-lit sign outside your restaurant—except this sign reaches thousands of potential diners online, right when they're hungry and ready to decide where to eat. For restaurants, being found easily in local searches is more than just helpful; it's essential for staying competitive in a world where most people rely on their phones to choose where to dine. Understanding local SEO is your first step toward taking control of how your business appears to those searchers.

The importance of local SEO lies in how search engines guide people to nearby options. A diner looking for "best burgers near me" or "family-friendly pizza" expects quick, accurate results that fit their needs. Restaurants that show up on the first page—especially at the top—gain the attention of these customers. The more visible your restaurant, the more likely you are to welcome those diners. This isn't just about luck or being popular; it's about understanding and using the tools and tactics that determine visibility.

One of the most powerful tools is Google My Business. It

serves as a digital storefront, offering diners essential details like your location, hours, and menu before they even visit your website. Done well, it doesn't just inform; it persuades. From glowing reviews to mouth-watering photos, your Google My Business profile can be the deciding factor in a customer's choice. But to maximize its potential, it needs to be set up and managed with care.

There are also many misconceptions about local SEO. Some believe it's only for big businesses with large budgets, while others think it's overly technical or hard to maintain. These ideas couldn't be further from the truth. Local SEO is accessible to every restaurant, no matter the size or location. With the right knowledge and effort, even small, family-owned spots can rank alongside—or above—well-known chains in search results.

Local SEO doesn't just get your name out there; it attracts diners who are already looking for what you offer. By connecting you with those who are ready to decide, it transforms your online presence into a steady flow of real-world customers. As you learn more, you'll see how small, focused efforts can lead to big rewards. This is the foundation of local SEO, and it's how your restaurant can stand out where it matters most.

What is Local SEO and Why Does It Matter?

In 2019, a small family-owned taco shop in Austin faced a challenge. Despite serving some of the best street tacos in the city, they struggled to bring in new customers. Their regulars loved them, but competition was fierce, and newer restaurants were capturing the attention of tourists and locals searching online. When they learned about local SEO, their fortunes shifted. By focusing on local search optimization, they appeared in the top results for "authentic tacos near me," driving foot traffic to their doors. In a few months, they saw a 40% increase in customers—a result of simply making themselves visible to people searching for exactly what they offered.

At its core, **local SEO is about showing up when someone nearby is looking for what you offer.** Unlike traditional SEO, which targets global rankings, local SEO focuses on helping businesses connect with nearby customers. For restaurants, this means ensuring your business appears in local search results for key phrases like "best brunch in [city]" or "family-friendly pizza near me." These results are often paired with a map and list of businesses—prime real estate for any restaurant looking to stand out.

For diners, search engines act as a digital compass. **People trust Google to guide them, often relying on its top suggestions.** This trust makes appearing in local search results a powerful way to capture interest and establish credibility. Think about the last time you searched for a restaurant. Did you scroll past the first few options? Most people don't. Studies show that 75% of users never click past the first page of search results. Ranking high in these results isn't just helpful; it's critical for restaurants that want to attract new customers.

What sets local SEO apart for restaurants is its ability to address specific customer needs in real time. When someone searches for "late-night eats near me," they aren't just browsing—they're ready to take action. **Local SEO connects you with these high-intent customers, giving you a competitive edge over restaurants that fail to optimize their pres-**

ence. Marcus Sheridan, author of *They Ask, You Answer*, emphasizes that addressing customer questions directly builds trust and visibility. Restaurants that understand and implement this approach don't just rank higher—they also earn customer loyalty by meeting their needs.

Beyond visibility, local SEO levels the playing field. Large chains often dominate traditional advertising with bigger budgets, but local SEO gives smaller restaurants a chance to compete. By targeting specific keywords and maintaining an optimized online presence, even a single-location eatery can outperform a national chain in local search results. This makes local SEO an accessible and impactful tool for restaurants of all sizes.

To make local SEO work, restaurants must understand what customers are looking for and ensure they're easy to find. This involves not only claiming and optimizing tools like Google My Business but also maintaining accurate information across all platforms. Consistency builds trust. For example, if your address or hours are incorrect on a platform like Yelp, potential diners might skip over you altogether. Every detail matters when it comes to creating a reliable and visible online presence.

Local SEO transforms your digital footprint into a customer magnet. By addressing queries like "vegetarian lunch spots near me," it positions your restaurant as the answer. It's not just about getting seen—it's about getting chosen. The ability to reach the right customers at the right time is what makes local SEO an invaluable strategy for restaurants in today's digital-first world.

How Local SEO Increases Visibility and Customer Traffic

Have you ever wondered why some restaurants are always bustling while others sit empty, even if they're just across the street from each other? The answer often lies in one thing: visibility. In today's world, search engines act as gate-keepers, and businesses that rank high in search results are far more likely to capture customer interest. For restaurants, being easily found in local searches directly translates into more diners walking through the door.

Search visibility isn't just about being noticed—it's about being chosen. When a potential diner searches for "best sushi near me," they're presented with a list of options. Studies show that 92% of searchers pick a business on the first page of results, and over 50% choose one of the top three listings. This means that where your restaurant ranks isn't just a matter of pride; it's a driving force for your foot traffic. The higher your ranking, the more likely it is that searchers will choose your restaurant over others.

Visibility is only part of the story. What truly sets high-ranking restaurants apart is their ability to connect with customers who are actively looking for what they offer. Local SEO ensures that when people search with intent—whether it's for "gluten-free pizza" or "cozy cafes downtown"—your business appears as a relevant and trustworthy option. **This trust is bolstered by features like accurate information, strong reviews, and compelling visuals that make customers feel confident about choosing you.**

To understand how visibility impacts your business, it's important to track measurable outcomes. Key metrics like search rankings, website traffic, and calls from Google My Business listings provide insight into how well your local SEO efforts are working. Tools like Google Analytics and

Google Search Console can show how many people are finding your restaurant through search and which keywords they're using. Additionally, tracking the number of new customers who mention finding you online gives you a tangible sense of local SEO's impact.

John Jantsch and Phil Singleton, authors of *SEO for Growth*, emphasize that measurable goals are vital for long-term success. By setting clear objectives—such as improving your search ranking for specific terms or increasing website traffic by a certain percentage—you create benchmarks to assess progress. **Regularly reviewing these metrics helps you adapt your strategy, ensuring consistent growth and visibility over time.**

Achieving high visibility takes effort, but it's far from unattainable. Start by optimizing your Google My Business profile, ensuring it includes accurate information, relevant keywords, and high-quality photos. Use local keywords strategically on your website, focusing on what sets your restaurant apart—whether it's your menu, ambiance, or unique offerings. These steps build trust with both search engines and potential customers, improving your chances of standing out.

The relationship between search visibility and customer traffic is clear: the more people see your restaurant in relevant searches, the more likely they are to visit. But it's not just about getting people in the door. A strong local SEO strategy creates a loop where satisfied customers leave positive reviews, which in turn boosts your rankings and visibility even further. This cycle of visibility, trust, and customer traffic is what makes local SEO an indispensable tool for any restaurant.

The Role of Google My Business in Local SEO

"Google My Business is your new homepage." This quote from local SEO expert Mike Blumenthal underscores just how vital this tool has become for businesses looking to thrive in a digital-first world. For restaurants, the importance of Google My Business (GMB) cannot be overstated. It's the first impression most potential diners will have of your establishment and serves as the primary gateway to your menu, location, and reviews. GMB is more than a listing—it's a dynamic platform that directly impacts search rankings, customer engagement, and ultimately, revenue.

At its core, GMB plays a pivotal role in local search rankings. When someone searches for "best Italian restaurants near me," Google pulls data from GMB profiles to populate its local pack—the highly visible section that shows top-rated businesses on a map. Restaurants with well-optimized profiles are far more likely to appear here, where the majority of clicks occur. Factors such as accurate contact details, relevant keywords in the business description, and frequent updates signal to Google that your profile is trustworthy and relevant. **Consistency is critical: discrepancies between your GMB profile and other online listings can lower your credibility, reducing your chances of appearing in these coveted spots.**

An optimized GMB profile doesn't just boost rankings; it drives engagement. Customers often decide where to eat based on the details they find here—hours of operation, photos, reviews, and even responses from the restaurant to previous customers. **Adding high-quality photos of your food, interior, and staff humanizes your business and entices potential diners.** According to Google, businesses with photos receive 42% more requests for directions and 35% more clicks to their websites compared to those without. This visual appeal, paired with complete and accurate information, can make the difference between a diner choosing you or scrolling to the next option.

Engagement doesn't stop with visuals. Reviews and direct communication through GMB also influence how customers perceive your restaurant. A steady flow of positive reviews not only improves your rankings but builds trust with potential diners. **Responding to these reviews—both positive and negative—shows that you value customer feedback and are willing to address concerns.** This transparency strengthens your brand image and creates a loyal customer base, as people are more likely to return to businesses that actively engage with their audience.

To maximize the benefits of GMB, active management is essential. Start by claiming your profile and ensuring all information—address, phone number, website, and hours—is accurate and up to date. Use your business description to highlight unique aspects of your restaurant, incorporating relevant local keywords like "vegan-friendly brunch in downtown Denver" or "authentic Thai cuisine in Boston." Keywords should flow naturally, enhancing the description without overwhelming it. **Regularly update your profile with posts about specials, events, or seasonal menu items to keep your content fresh and engaging.**

The insights provided by GMB are another invaluable resource. The platform offers data on how customers interact with your profile, including how they found you, what actions they took, and where they're located. This information allows you to refine your strategy by identifying which aspects of your listing resonate most with your audience. For example, if your photos consistently attract views but fewer people click on your menu, consider adjusting how your dishes are described or adding more enticing imagery. **Tracking these metrics ensures you're not just visible, but impactful.**

GMB also integrates seamlessly with other aspects of local SEO, acting as the foundation of a cohesive online presence. When paired with consistent citations across directories, a strong review management strategy, and effective keyword optimization, your GMB profile amplifies the impact of your efforts. Blumenthal and Mihm, in their book *Local SEO Secrets*, emphasize that treating GMB as an active tool rather than a static listing gives restaurants an edge in a competitive market. **It's not enough to set up your profile and walk away —regular engagement is what keeps your business top-of-mind for both Google and your customers.**

Every detail within your GMB profile serves a purpose, from the precision of your business name to the vibrancy of your photos. By focusing on accuracy, relevancy, and engagement, you position your restaurant as a trusted, visible option in the crowded digital landscape. With GMB as the cornerstone of your local SEO strategy, you don't just get found— you get chosen.

Debunking Myths About Local SEO for Restaurants

"Negative reviews are a gift—an opportunity to show how much you care." This insight from Tony Langham, a leading voice in reputation management, challenges one of the most persistent myths about online feedback. Many restaurant owners dread seeing a less-than-stellar review, assuming it will scare away potential customers. The truth is, how you respond matters far more than the review itself. Thoughtful replies can not only repair trust with the original customer but also impress future diners who see your willingness to address concerns openly. This shift in perspective is just one of many myths about local SEO that need to be unraveled.

One common misconception is that managing local SEO requires advanced technical skills. Restaurant owners often imagine coding, complex algorithms, or hours spent tinkering with websites. In reality, most local SEO tasks—like updating your Google My Business profile or asking for customer reviews—require no more than a basic understanding of your business's online tools. Platforms like Google and Yelp are designed to be user-friendly, with straightforward instructions for adding details like hours, photos, or menu links. **What matters most is consistency and attention to detail, not technical expertise.**

Another myth is that improving local SEO is prohibitively expensive. While hiring an expert can be helpful, many impactful strategies are completely free. Claiming your Google My Business profile, responding to reviews, and optimizing your website for local keywords are all steps you can take without spending a dime. Investing time rather than money often yields significant returns. For example, adding photos of your signature dishes or running a social media promotion that links to your GMB page can drive immediate results without additional costs.

Local SEO is also more effective than many realize. Some restaurant owners believe it's only relevant for big businesses or trendy locations. This couldn't be further from the truth. **Search engines prioritize relevance and proximity, meaning a well-optimized family diner can outrank a larger chain simply by having accurate, engaging, and locally focused**

content. Small, thoughtful efforts—like adding a keyword-rich description to your online listings—can have an outsized impact.

One of the most overlooked aspects of local SEO is its ability to transform negative reviews into opportunities for growth. When a customer voices a complaint online, responding with empathy and a clear solution not only helps the individual but also reassures others that your business values its patrons. A response like, "We're sorry to hear about your experience—let us make it right," shows accountability and a willingness to improve. **This transparency can make potential diners feel confident choosing your restaurant, even if the review itself wasn't glowing.**

Reputation management ties directly into local SEO, as search engines take customer reviews into account when ranking businesses. A steady stream of positive feedback tells Google that your restaurant is well-regarded, improving your chances of appearing in top search results. However, it's not just about the volume of reviews; their content and your responses matter, too. Engaged, professional replies can amplify the impact of your existing reviews, helping you build trust with customers and algorithms alike.

Finally, local SEO is a dynamic process, not a one-time fix. Many believe that optimizing their online presence once is enough to maintain visibility indefinitely. The reality is that search engines favor fresh, updated content. Regularly posting new photos, keeping your menu current, and updating seasonal hours ensure that your listings remain relevant. **This ongoing attention signals to both search engines and customers that your business is active and ready to serve.**

As myths about local SEO fade, what remains is a clearer

picture of its potential to elevate restaurants of all sizes. By focusing on simple, accessible strategies—accurate listings, active engagement with reviews, and consistent updates—you can transform your online presence into a powerful driver of customer trust and traffic.

CHAPTER 2
CLAIMING AND OPTIMIZING YOUR GOOGLE MY BUSINESS PROFILE

GET YOUR RESTAURANT FOUND ONLINE WITH A WINNING GMB STRATEGY

Imagine a couple planning their anniversary dinner, phones in hand, searching for "romantic Italian restaurants nearby." The search results display a few options, but one listing catches their eye: it has glowing reviews, inviting photos of candlelit tables, and even highlights tonight's special—a handmade pasta dish. They make their reservation on the spot, all before leaving the search page. This seamless decision-making process, driven by a strong Google My Business profile, is a perfect example of how this tool connects restaurants with eager customers in real time.

Google My Business is more than just an online listing. It acts as a central hub for your restaurant's digital presence, providing everything potential diners need to decide if your spot is the right fit. Unlike a website, which customers must actively visit, GMB delivers key information directly within search results and maps, placing your restaurant front and center where decisions are made. **A fully optimized profile not only ensures you're visible to local searchers but also**

builds trust by presenting accurate, engaging details about your business.

The significance of GMB goes beyond visibility. Search engines favor businesses with complete, consistent, and frequently updated profiles, which means optimizing your GMB doesn't just help customers—it improves your search ranking. This ranking isn't determined by luck but by specific signals, like having your menu linked, your hours accurately displayed, and your photos reflecting the quality of your offerings. These details help Google understand that your restaurant is relevant and reliable, giving you a better chance to appear in the coveted top spots.

But GMB isn't just a tool for search engines; it's a direct line of communication with your audience. Customers can leave reviews, ask questions, or even message you directly. **Every interaction, from answering a review to posting about an upcoming event, strengthens your relationship with both existing patrons and new visitors.** This engagement doesn't just enhance their experience; it signals to others that your restaurant is active and attentive, setting you apart from competitors who neglect their profiles.

Claiming and optimizing your Google My Business profile is the foundation of any successful local SEO strategy. It ensures that the information diners see when they search is accurate and compelling, giving them the confidence to choose your restaurant over others. Whether it's a detailed description of your atmosphere or high-quality images of your most popular dishes, every element of your profile is an opportunity to connect with your ideal customer. With the right approach, GMB becomes more than just a listing—it becomes a powerful driver of trust, visibility, and traffic.

Setting Up and Verifying Your Google My Business Profile

When a neighborhood coffee shop in Seattle opened its doors, they assumed their regulars would keep the business afloat. Yet, as the months passed, foot traffic lagged, and the owners struggled to attract new customers. That changed when they set up their Google My Business profile. Within weeks of verifying their listing and adding photos of their cozy seating and pastries, their shop became a top result for "best coffee near me." The result? A steady stream of new faces and increased sales. This transformation highlights the power of a properly set up and verified GMB profile.

The process begins with claiming your profile. Start by navigating to the Google My Business homepage and searching for your restaurant to check if a listing already exists. If it does, you'll have the option to claim it, provided you verify your connection to the business. For new businesses, creating a listing involves entering essential details such as your restaurant's name, address, phone number, website, and hours of operation. Accuracy is critical at this stage—any discrepancies in this data can confuse customers and hinder your search ranking.

Verification is the next step and arguably the most crucial. Google offers multiple verification methods, but the most common is via a postcard mailed to your business address. This postcard contains a unique code that you'll need to enter online to confirm your ownership. While this method is straightforward, delays or lost postcards can complicate the process. To avoid issues, double-check that your address is correct and accessible. For businesses in unique situations— like operating from a shared space or lacking a traditional storefront—alternative methods, such as email or phone verification, may be available.

One common pitfall during setup is incomplete information. For instance, failing to specify your business category or neglecting to add service areas can limit your profile's effectiveness. Choosing the right category—like "Italian restaurant" or "casual dining"—helps Google connect you with relevant searchers. Additionally, adding service areas is essential if your restaurant offers delivery or caters to specific neighborhoods. These details ensure that your profile is as visible and relevant as possible.

Another challenge arises with verification. If the postcard doesn't arrive, contacting Google support is the fastest way to resolve the issue. They can reissue the card or offer alternative verification methods. For businesses in shared buildings or rural areas, where mail delivery can be unreliable, verifying through email or phone is often the better option. Regularly checking Google's support updates ensures you're aware of the latest options available.

Once your GMB profile is verified, optimizing it immediately maximizes its impact. Begin by adding high-quality photos that showcase your restaurant's atmosphere and menu. Clear, vibrant images of your dishes and dining spaces create a strong visual impression and attract more clicks. Including a detailed business description with locally relevant keywords—such as "family-friendly BBQ in Houston"—further strengthens your profile. Google prioritizes listings that engage with users, so every update you make signals that your business is active and ready to welcome diners.

For many restaurant owners, the technical details of setting up and verifying a GMB profile may seem intimidating. Yet the tools and support Google provides make the process manageable even for beginners. By focusing on accuracy, verification, and ongoing updates, you set the foundation for a robust online presence. Your GMB profile becomes more than just a listing—it transforms into a vital connection point between your restaurant and the diners searching for their next great meal.

Filling Out Essential Information to Maximize Visibility

Have you ever searched online for a business, only to find the address or hours of operation were wrong? That moment of frustration often leads to a quick decision to move on to a competitor. For restaurants, these small details can make or break whether someone walks through your doors or chooses the place next door. Filling out and maintaining accurate, detailed information on your Google My Business (GMB) profile isn't just a chore—it's a strategy that directly impacts your visibility and credibility.

The foundation of a successful GMB profile begins with ensuring that every piece of information is correct and consistent. **Your address, phone number, hours of operation, and website URL should match exactly across all platforms, including your website and social media.** This consistency builds trust with both search engines and potential customers. Search engines rely on this accuracy to determine the legitimacy of your business, while customers feel more confident when they find the same details wherever they look.

One overlooked element is the business category. Google uses this to connect your restaurant with the most relevant searches. Choosing the wrong category—like "café" instead of "seafood restaurant"—can lead to missed opportunities.

Specificity is key. If your restaurant specializes in vegan Mexican cuisine, selecting categories that highlight these niches not only improves your visibility but also attracts diners looking for exactly what you offer.

Equally important is optimizing the description on your profile. This short piece of text is your chance to tell potential customers what makes your restaurant unique. **Use locally relevant keywords in your description to boost your chances of appearing in search results.** For example, phrases like "locally-sourced farm-to-table in Portland" or "best BBQ ribs in Austin" align your profile with common search terms. These keywords don't just increase visibility; they set the tone for the type of experience customers can expect.

Consistency doesn't stop with basic information. Your menu should also reflect accurate and up-to-date offerings. Linking your menu directly to your GMB profile ensures that searchers see a clear picture of what you offer. Better yet, if your menu includes items tailored to local tastes—like regional specialties or seasonal dishes—mentioning them in your menu descriptions adds another layer of local SEO value. **Restaurants that emphasize their connection to the local community often see higher engagement, as diners are drawn to businesses that resonate with their surroundings.**

Maintaining consistency across platforms is about more than looking professional. It directly impacts your local SEO rankings. When Google sees that your business details are aligned everywhere—on your GMB profile, Yelp, TripAdvisor, and your website—it assigns higher credibility to your business. This credibility translates to better placement in search results, increasing your visibility to potential diners.

Filling out every field in your GMB profile may seem tedious, but the benefits are undeniable. Every accurate detail strengthens your position in the competitive online space, where even small inconsistencies can erode trust. By aligning your profile with your broader online presence and thoughtfully incorporating keywords that reflect your unique offerings, you'll not only improve visibility but also create a seamless, trustworthy experience for your customers from their first search to their first bite.

Leveraging Photos and Videos to Attract Diners

When someone scrolls through an online listing and sees a beautifully plated dish glistening under natural light, their next thought is often, "I have to try that." Studies have shown that businesses with high-quality images on their Google My Business (GMB) profiles receive 42% more requests for directions and 35% more clicks to their websites, according to Google. Visual content isn't just a nice addition—it's one of the most compelling tools for attracting diners and building trust.

The power of photos lies in their ability to communicate your brand instantly. A picture of a sizzling steak or a vibrant, freshly tossed salad conveys a sensory experience that words cannot match. However, for this impact to work, the quality of the photos must reflect the quality of the dining experience. **Images should be clear, well-lit, and free from clutter.** Blurry, poorly framed shots can create doubt about the professionalism of your restaurant. A smartphone with a good camera, combined with simple editing apps like Snapseed, can yield excellent results if you follow a few best practices. Use natural light whenever possible, avoid busy backgrounds, and focus on vibrant colors that pop.

Adding videos to your profile is another effective strategy. Videos can show the atmosphere of your space, the energy of your staff, or the care that goes into preparing dishes. A short, 15-second clip of your chef drizzling sauce over a dish can be more engaging than a static image. Tools like Canva or Adobe Spark make it easy to create polished video content without advanced skills. Regularly updating this content ensures that potential diners always see fresh, relevant visuals, whether it's a new seasonal dish or a special event.

Consistency in uploading new photos and videos signals to Google and to users that your business is active and attentive. Profiles with recent uploads tend to perform better in local searches because Google rewards active engagement. This is especially critical for restaurants competing in crowded markets. A vibrant, up-to-date profile stands out in search results and leaves a lasting impression on viewers.

Strategic placement of visuals can amplify their impact. Use photos to highlight your strengths. If your restaurant boasts a stunning outdoor patio, include shots that showcase it during golden hour. For a bakery, close-ups of frosted cupcakes or artisan bread fresh from the oven can evoke an irresistible craving. Beyond the visuals, add brief, keyword-rich captions to describe what's in the photo or video. Phrases like "house-smoked brisket with tangy BBQ sauce" not only entice diners but also boost your profile's SEO by aligning with search queries.

While quality is key, volume also plays a role. A GMB profile with a robust collection of images covering various aspects—menu items, the interior and exterior of the restaurant, and staff interactions—creates a comprehensive virtual experience for potential customers. People often look for authenticity, so don't hesitate to include candid moments, such as a smiling server delivering a dish or a happy diner enjoying their meal.

High-quality visuals are not a one-time effort. Regular updates keep your profile fresh and engaging. Make a habit of photographing new menu items, special events, or even daily operations. By consistently sharing content that reflects your restaurant's personality and offerings, you'll create a profile that not only attracts diners but also builds trust and anticipation.

Managing Google My Business Insights for Better Decision-Making

"How do your customers find you?" It's a simple question with a complex answer hidden in the data. Google My Business (GMB) Insights provides a treasure trove of information that can help you understand how people discover and interact with your business online. The real power of this data lies in turning it into actionable strategies that enhance your visibility and grow your customer base.

At its core, GMB Insights reveals how your business appears in search results and what actions customers take after finding you. One of the most revealing metrics is customer search terms. These show the exact words and phrases people use to find your restaurant. If "best brunch near me" or "gluten-free pizza options" consistently appears, it signals an opportunity to align your descriptions and posts with these terms. Incorporating these phrases into your GMB profile can help reinforce your relevance and improve your ranking in future searches.

Engagement data is equally illuminating. Pay attention to metrics like the number of phone calls, requests for directions, and website clicks. For example, if there's a spike in calls every Saturday morning, this might reflect a growing interest in your weekend breakfast menu. Conversely, if direction requests drop off during certain hours, it may indicate confusion about your operating times or lack of appeal in those time slots. Adjusting your messaging or promotions around this feedback can lead to more consistent foot traffic.

Another key insight is how often your business appears in searches versus how often people interact with it. A high number of views but low engagement could mean your profile isn't enticing enough. This might be due to outdated photos, incomplete information, or weak descriptions. Updating your visuals, ensuring your menu is current, and using keywords that resonate with your audience can address this gap effectively.

Consistency across all your platforms amplifies the trustworthiness of your profile. Insights can highlight discrepancies in your business information. If your GMB profile shows different hours from your website or social media pages, customers may lose confidence. Ensuring alignment across all listings is critical for maintaining credibility and preventing lost opportunities. Tools like BrightLocal or Yext can streamline this process by helping you manage multiple listings efficiently.

GMB Insights also sheds light on the performance of specific posts and promotions. If you frequently share updates about limited-time offers, examining the engagement rates of these posts can guide future campaigns. For instance, a high click-through rate on a post about a Valentine's Day special suggests that customers respond well to holiday-themed promotions. This data-driven feedback loop enables you to fine-tune your marketing strategies for maximum impact.

Location-based insights provide additional layers of understanding. If most direction requests come from a specific neighborhood, consider targeted advertising in that area. Similarly, if a neighboring city rarely shows up in your data, it might be worth exploring why your business isn't reaching those potential diners. Adjusting your radius for delivery or running geo-targeted ads can bridge these gaps.

Analyzing trends over time can help you anticipate future needs. For instance, if there's a steady increase in direction requests during warmer months, outdoor seating could be a significant draw. This proactive use of insights allows you to make decisions that align with customer preferences, ensuring you're always one step ahead.

Ultimately, GMB Insights isn't just about collecting data— it's about using that data to craft a strategy that resonates with your audience. By interpreting these analytics thoughtfully, you can uncover patterns, correct weak points, and focus your efforts on the tactics that truly work. This thoughtful approach to managing your profile turns what could be a static listing into a dynamic tool for growth.

CHAPTER 3
MASTERING LOCAL KEYWORD RESEARCH

DISCOVER THE SEARCH PHRASES THAT DRIVE DINERS TO YOUR DOOR

What makes someone search for "best Italian restaurant near me" instead of just "Italian food"? The answer lies in understanding how people think when they use search engines. Local keyword research reveals these patterns, offering insights into what customers want and how they express it. By mastering this skill, restaurants can attract diners at the exact moment they're ready to make a decision.

Every keyword tells a story about customer intent. Some terms, like "pizza delivery," suggest urgency, while others, such as "romantic dining in the city," indicate someone planning an experience. Understanding this difference allows businesses to tailor their messaging, ensuring it aligns with the specific needs of potential customers. When these insights guide your content, your restaurant appears in searches that matter most.

Precision is critical. The right keywords connect your business to nearby diners searching for exactly what you offer. For example, a café in downtown Austin will benefit more from "downtown Austin coffee shops" than generic terms like "coffee." Hyperlocal phrases capture searches from those most likely to visit, making your marketing efforts more effective. The process starts with discovering these specific terms and then strategically using them to boost visibility.

Keyword research also brings surprises. Many restaurants learn that potential customers use unexpected terms to describe their offerings. A family-friendly diner might discover that people search for "kid-friendly brunch spots" or "restaurants with high chairs." Identifying these hidden opportunities can open new doors to customer engagement and help differentiate your business from competitors.

Another key element is the evolving nature of search behavior. Voice assistants like Alexa and Siri have changed how people search. Instead of typing "cheap sushi," they might ask, "Where can I find affordable sushi nearby?" Researching these conversational queries ensures your restaurant stays relevant in a shifting digital landscape.

The work doesn't end once you've found your keywords. Tracking how these terms perform over time allows you to adjust your strategy. If a once-popular search phrase declines in use, it might signal a shift in customer preferences or competition. By continually refining your keyword list, you can stay ahead of trends and maintain a strong connection with your audience.

At its core, local keyword research is about understanding your community and using that knowledge to make your business visible where it matters most. From capturing new diners to keeping regulars engaged, the phrases you choose can make a significant impact on your restaurant's success. This foundational understanding sets the stage for exploring how to identify, implement, and maximize the power of local keywords.

Why Keywords Are Critical for Local SEO Success

Imagine a neighborhood coffee shop struggling to compete with a national chain that just opened down the block. Despite offering better coffee and a cozier atmosphere, the shop's sales began to dip. What changed everything wasn't a flashy ad campaign or a new drink on the menu—it was identifying the search term "best coffee near Main Street." By incorporating this keyword into its website and Google My Business profile, the shop began attracting locals searching online for a perfect cup. The keyword wasn't just a phrase; it was a connection to the exact customers who needed what the shop had to offer.

Keywords are the foundation of search engine optimization because they match the language businesses use to the terms their customers search for. They help search engines understand the content on your website and decide when to display your business in search results. Broad keywords, like "pizza," might attract a global audience, but local keywords, such as "wood-fired pizza in Brooklyn," zero in on the people most likely to visit your restaurant. **Focusing on local keywords ensures your marketing efforts reach the diners who are nearby and actively looking for your offerings.**

The intent behind a search term adds another layer of importance to keyword selection. Someone typing "late-night tacos near me" likely wants an immediate answer to a craving, while a search like "best taco spots for birthdays" suggests planning for an event. Search intent drives how you approach your content strategy. **For example, you could create blog posts about your extended hours to address late-night cravings or showcase party packages to appeal to** planners. **Understanding intent ensures that your content is relevant and resonates with your audience.**

A successful keyword strategy doesn't stop at simply selecting phrases. It weaves those keywords into your website, menus, and online profiles in a way that feels natural and informative. **Aligning keyword use with content marketing is crucial to staying competitive. According to "SEO for Growth" by John Jantsch and Phil Singleton, content that meets audience needs while leveraging well-researched keywords creates the trust and visibility that drive results.** When your menu descriptions, blog articles, and social media posts speak the same language as your audience, search engines reward you by making your business more visible.

Broad keywords have their place but often serve larger chains or general informational content. Local businesses thrive when they can outcompete bigger names by being specific. This specificity not only narrows competition but also makes your business more relevant to those nearby. A diner doesn't need to know about the top-rated burger joint across the country—they need to find the juiciest burger five blocks away. **This distinction makes the strategic use of local keywords a non-negotiable for small businesses aiming to dominate their local market.**

When you focus on keywords that align with customer intent, your efforts are amplified. You're not just attracting any traffic; you're attracting the right traffic—people who are ready to engage with what you have to offer. By understanding what these phrases mean and why they matter, you're equipped to build a foundation of trust and relevance that extends far beyond the search results page.

Finding High-Impact Keywords for Your Restaurant

How can your restaurant stand out when potential diners search online? The answer lies in uncovering the exact phrases they're typing into search bars. High-impact keywords act as a bridge between what your business offers and what people are actively looking for. Tools like Google Keyword Planner and UberSuggest can reveal these phrases, helping you identify terms that bring your audience directly to your digital doorstep.

Google Keyword Planner is one of the most powerful tools for discovering valuable keywords. It allows you to input basic terms related to your cuisine, services, or location and provides a list of suggestions along with important metrics like search volume and competition level. For example, a sushi restaurant in Austin might input "sushi" and uncover terms like "sushi bar downtown Austin" or "fresh sushi near me," which may have lower competition but high relevance. **Focusing on these specific terms helps you optimize your website and online profiles for visibility where it matters most.**

UberSuggest, on the other hand, excels at uncovering niche terms and long-tail keywords—those longer, highly specific phrases often overlooked by competitors. These keywords may attract fewer searches individually but are incredibly effective at connecting with users who are ready to take action. A restaurant specializing in vegan Mexican cuisine might discover phrases like "vegan taco trucks in Los Angeles" or "best plant-based enchiladas near Hollywood." **Because long-tail keywords tend to reflect clear intent, they are especially useful for capturing a more motivated audience.**

Identifying niche terms can set your business apart. If your menu includes regional or specialty items, such as Georgian khachapuri or Korean bingsu, integrating these terms into your website or Google My Business profile ensures you capture diners looking for those exact dishes. Even within more common cuisines, being specific about preparation styles or unique offerings can make a big difference. **Rather than relying on broad terms like "Italian restaurant," focus on phrases like "handmade pasta in Denver" or "wood-fired Neapolitan pizza in San Francisco." This level of specificity not only helps your ranking but also appeals to diners looking for exactly what you provide.**

Search intent is the key to understanding which keywords are worth targeting. A search for "romantic steakhouse in Chicago" suggests someone planning a special night out, whereas "steakhouse delivery near me" points to someone who wants a quick, satisfying meal at home. Recognizing this intent allows you to align your content with customer needs. **For example, you might feature elegant photos and date-night recommendations to cater to one audience while highlighting takeout deals or speed of service for another. Each keyword has its role, and the context in which it's used matters.**

Using keyword tools effectively also means evaluating the data these tools provide. High search volume indicates popularity, but keywords with moderate or lower competition can offer better opportunities, especially for small or independent restaurants. **Balancing search volume, competition level, and intent ensures you target terms that can actually make a difference for your business.**

By focusing on tools like Google Keyword Planner and UberSuggest, honing in on niche terms, and prioritizing long-tail keywords with clear intent, you create a strategy that connects your restaurant to the exact customers searching for it. These insights don't just boost your visibility—they ensure that your visibility translates to real-world foot traffic and loyal patrons.

Incorporating Keywords into Your Digital Presence

"Keywords are the currency of online visibility," said marketing strategist John Jantsch in *SEO for Growth*. This simple yet powerful observation underscores the role of thoughtful keyword placement in a restaurant's digital presence. It's not enough to know your audience's search terms; success lies in how and where those keywords are integrated across your platforms. Done right, keywords can guide diners directly to your table. Done poorly, they can make your content look robotic or out of touch.

Strategic keyword placement begins with your Google My Business (GMB) profile, the hub of your online identity. Your description should seamlessly weave high-impact keywords into a natural and engaging narrative about your restaurant. For example, instead of a generic phrase like "We serve the best pizza," opt for "Our wood-fired Margherita pizza is a favorite among downtown Brooklyn diners." **This approach highlights both the unique appeal of your offering and the local area, boosting relevance in search results.**

Menus are another key area for incorporating keywords. Beyond simply listing dishes, use descriptive phrases that reflect popular search terms. For instance, if "vegan Thai food in Austin" is a trending search in your area, ensure your menu includes detailed descriptions like "Vegan Pad Thai with organic tofu and tamarind sauce." **The specificity not** only helps search engines but also creates a richer experience for potential diners, showcasing the care and thought you put into your offerings.

Posts on GMB and social media present regular opportunities to reinforce your keywords without overloading your content. Share updates about seasonal specials, local partnerships, or events, naturally including keywords as part of the narrative. For instance, a bakery could post, "Excited to share our gluten-free pumpkin muffins at the downtown farmers market this weekend!" **This type of post resonates with both human readers and search engines, amplifying engagement and discoverability.**

While keywords are essential, overusing them—or "stuffing"—can harm both your ranking and your reputation. Search engines penalize content that appears spammy or artificial, and customers can quickly lose trust in a brand that prioritizes algorithms over authentic communication. **The key is balance: use keywords sparingly and in context, always prioritizing clarity and value for your audience.**

Consistency across platforms is critical for building credibility. Whether on your website, GMB profile, or social media accounts, ensure that the language, tone, and key terms align. This coherence helps search engines associate your brand with specific keywords and builds trust with customers who encounter a unified message at every touchpoint. **For example, if your website highlights "authentic Neapolitan pizza," your GMB profile and Instagram should use the same phrase rather than variations like "traditional Italian pizza."**

Implementing keywords effectively requires a blend of strategy and creativity. It's about finding the right words and placing them where they can have the most impact, all while maintaining an authentic voice. By focusing on quality and context, you ensure your digital presence not only attracts diners but also keeps them engaged.

Tracking and Updating Your Keyword Strategy

"Trends change, and so should your strategy," says Phil Singleton in *SEO for Growth,* a reminder that staying relevant in the online world requires continuous effort. Keywords that bring customers through your door today might not work as effectively tomorrow. Monitoring their performance and making timely updates is the foundation of a successful keyword strategy. Without consistent evaluation, even the most carefully chosen keywords can lose their impact over time.

Tracking the effectiveness of your keywords begins with understanding the metrics that matter. Tools like Google Analytics and Google Search Console provide valuable insights into how users discover your restaurant. Pay close attention to metrics like **impressions, click-through rates (CTR), and average position in search results**. These numbers reveal not only which keywords are driving traffic but also how well your content resonates with users' needs.

Adjusting your strategy based on performance data ensures that your efforts align with what customers are actively searching for. If data shows a decline in searches for a specific keyword, it might indicate a shift in trends or preferences. For example, if "farm-to-table brunch" sees a drop in interest, it may be time to focus on other aspects of your menu, like seasonal specials or regional flavors that are gaining popularity. **Adaptation is key to maintaining visi-**

bility and staying relevant to your audience's evolving tastes.

Seasonal patterns also play a significant role in keyword performance. Terms like "cozy winter meals" or "outdoor dining near me" naturally spike during specific times of the year. Aligning your content with these fluctuations not only boosts engagement but also positions your restaurant as in tune with customer expectations. Regularly reviewing trends through platforms like Google Trends helps identify these opportunities and informs timely adjustments.

Streamlining the tracking and updating process is easier with the right tools. Paid platforms like SEMrush and Ahrefs offer detailed keyword analysis, competitor insights, and suggestions for untapped opportunities. For a more budget-friendly option, Google's Keyword Planner provides essential data to refine your approach. **These tools automate much of the heavy lifting, allowing you to focus on crafting content that reflects the keywords most likely to drive results.**

Finally, an effective keyword strategy is not static. It thrives on iteration and feedback. Incorporating new keywords inspired by customer reviews, social media interactions, or menu changes ensures your strategy remains dynamic and responsive. **This proactive approach strengthens your online presence and builds lasting connections with diners.**

Through careful monitoring, timely adjustments, and the strategic use of tools, you can transform keyword data into actionable insights. This ongoing process not only optimizes your digital presence but also ensures it continues to reflect the changing desires of your audience.

CHAPTER 4
BUILDING LOCAL CITATIONS AND CONSISTENT LISTINGS

INCREASE YOUR ONLINE AUTHORITY WITH RELIABLE BUSINESS LISTINGS

How do customers decide where to eat? Increasingly, it's based on what they find online. Reliable business listings across platforms like Google, Yelp, and local directories act as a restaurant's digital handshake, introducing it to potential diners and building trust. These listings, known as local citations, are far more than just basic contact details—they are signals of credibility that influence how search engines rank businesses in local results. Without accurate and consistent information, even the most beloved local spot might struggle to compete for attention.

A strong foundation of local citations begins with ensuring that the **name, address, and phone number (NAP)** are correct and identical across every platform. Search engines prioritize reliability, and inconsistencies—no matter how minor—can confuse algorithms and diminish a business's visibility. For restaurants, this could mean missing out on being featured in searches for "best pizza near me" or "family-friendly dining in [city]." Accuracy here is not just helpful for search engines—it directly affects customer trust.

Imagine a diner calling a listed number only to find it out of service or arriving at an incorrect location.

Consistency goes beyond the basics. Incorporating keywords naturally into business descriptions, menus, and services further strengthens a restaurant's online presence. A listing that highlights "authentic Mexican cuisine" or "vegan-friendly brunch options" not only helps customers but also aligns with how they are searching. When repeated consistently across directories, this information creates a web of relevance that search engines use to determine the business's authority in its niche.

Maintaining local citations is not a one-time effort. Businesses need to monitor and update their listings regularly to reflect changes, whether it's a new phone number, updated hours, or seasonal menu shifts. This ensures not only accuracy but also that the business remains relevant to evolving customer expectations. Tools like BrightLocal and Moz Local simplify this process, enabling restaurants to track their citations and address any discrepancies efficiently.

As the foundation for a restaurant's digital presence, local citations and consistent listings create a seamless connection between online discovery and real-world dining. By ensuring that every detail aligns across platforms, restaurants establish themselves as trustworthy, relevant, and ready to welcome new customers.

What Are Local Citations and Why Are They Important?

Imagine a customer searching online for "vegan brunch near me" and discovering a nearby café with glowing reviews and clear contact details. That connection didn't happen by chance. It was the result of an invisible yet powerful tool:

local citations. These digital mentions of a business's name, address, and phone number (NAP) across directories, websites, and social platforms create a foundation for being found online. Without them, even the best restaurants can remain invisible to their audience.

At its core, a local citation is a mention of a business's NAP information in places like Google Business Profiles, Yelp, and niche directories such as OpenTable or Zomato. These citations are more than simple listings—they are trust signals that search engines use to verify a business's credibility. Accurate and consistent citations tell algorithms, "This is a legitimate business," which increases its chances of appearing in local search results. For restaurants, this can mean being the first option potential diners see when they're deciding where to eat.

Consistency is the backbone of effective citations. If your restaurant is listed as "Joe's Italian Bistro" on one site but "Joe's Authentic Italian" on another, search engines may struggle to understand if they're the same place. Even small discrepancies, like an outdated phone number or a missing suite number, can weaken a citation's power. **Ensuring every listing reflects the exact same details—down to abbreviations like "St." versus "Street"—is critical for building trust with both search engines and customers.**

Authoritative listing sites play a key role in citation-building. Platforms like Google Maps and Yelp are well-known for their influence on local search, but niche directories carry significant weight too. A seafood restaurant, for example, benefits from a listing on a site like SeafoodSource, which adds industry relevance. Similarly, regional directories and tourism websites provide localized authority that boosts visibility in specific markets. Each listing acts as a digital breadcrumb leading potential customers directly to your door.

The importance of local citations doesn't stop with initial setup. As a business grows or its details change, maintaining up-to-date information ensures continued relevance. This dynamic nature means that citations must be treated as a living part of your digital strategy. Whether using tools like Moz Local to audit and manage listings or manually updating key directories, a focus on accuracy and consistency keeps your business positioned as a reliable choice for customers searching online.

Creating Citations for Your Restaurant

Did you know that having your restaurant listed on just one trusted directory can increase your chances of being discovered online by as much as 50%? Now imagine amplifying that effect with multiple, accurate listings across the web. This is the power of creating local citations for your restaurant—laying the groundwork for consistent visibility where it matters most.

Creating effective citations starts with a clear understanding of what they represent. A citation is not just a mention of your business; it is a digital handshake between your restaurant and potential customers. Each entry acts as an introduction, providing essential details such as your name, address, and phone number (NAP), as well as key enhancements like your website link, hours of operation, and a brief description of your offerings. To maximize this impact, **each citation must be precise and uniform across platforms. A single inconsistency can dilute your online presence and create confusion for both search engines and customers.**

Building new citations involves a methodical approach. Start by identifying reputable platforms where your restaurant should be listed. Well-known directories like Yelp, TripAdvisor, and Google Business Profile are must-haves. But don't overlook niche platforms tailored to the food industry, such as OpenTable, Zomato, and Resy, which can attract diners with specific preferences or needs. Once these core platforms are established, consider opportunities on regional directories and local tourism sites, which can help your restaurant connect with people searching for dining options in your area.

Accuracy is crucial when setting up your citations. Every detail matters, from how your business name appears to the exact spelling of your street address. Using a single, standard format ensures consistency. For instance, decide early whether to abbreviate "Street" as "St." or spell it out, and stick to that decision everywhere. **This uniformity sends a strong signal to search engines, boosting your credibility and improving your local SEO rankings.**

Duplicate or outdated listings are among the most common pitfalls in citation management. A duplicate listing can occur when your business undergoes changes, such as a new phone number or location, and older entries remain active online. These discrepancies confuse algorithms and undermine your SEO efforts. Use tools like Moz Local or BrightLocal to audit your existing citations and identify duplicates or inaccuracies. Once identified, correct or remove them promptly to avoid conflicts.

Opportunities for citations extend beyond the obvious directories. Think about partnerships with local bloggers, sponsorship mentions on community websites, or even reviews in regional food publications. These non-traditional citations can carry significant weight, especially when they align with your restaurant's identity and values. For example, a farm-to-table bistro might benefit from being listed on a sustainability-focused directory, while a late-night diner could prioritize inclusion in nightlife guides.

Creating citations is not a one-time task. It's an ongoing effort to maintain your restaurant's relevance and visibility in a competitive market. By starting with a solid foundation and focusing on accuracy, consistency, and strategic placements, you set the stage for stronger connections with both diners and search engines.

Auditing and Fixing Existing Business Listings

"When was the last time you checked if your online listings reflect who you are today?" Businesses evolve, yet many fail to update their digital footprints, leaving outdated information scattered across the web. For restaurants, where accurate details are essential for bookings and customer trust, these inaccuracies can cost more than just SEO rankings—they can erode credibility with diners who rely on consistent details to make decisions.

Auditing your existing citations begins with a thorough sweep of where your business is currently listed. Tools like Moz Local and BrightLocal are excellent resources for identifying the listings tied to your restaurant. These tools comb through directories to reveal inconsistencies in key details, such as your name, address, phone number (NAP), or operating hours. The results often highlight duplicates, conflicting information, and even listings you may have forgotten existed. **Your goal in this process is to ensure every online mention of your restaurant matches exactly, word for word,** across platforms. **Consistency reinforces trust and signals authority to search engines like Google.**

Once the errors have been identified, managing corrections efficiently requires prioritization. Start with the most visible platforms—Google Business Profile, Yelp, and TripAdvisor—and confirm your details are accurate. These sites drive significant traffic and are often the first places customers look for your business. Corrections on less prominent directories can follow, but remember, each listing matters in creating a cohesive online presence. For managing changes at scale, services like Yext can automate updates across dozens of platforms, ensuring uniformity with minimal effort.

Monitoring your listings for ongoing consistency is not a one-time task; it's a maintenance commitment. Every time your restaurant undergoes a change, whether it's a phone number, new hours, or even a slight rebranding, those changes must be reflected across all citations. Missing even a single update can lead to customer frustration and lower rankings. **Regular checks—perhaps quarterly—help catch issues before they snowball into larger problems. Tools like SEMrush or Ahrefs can simplify this process by tracking your listings and alerting you to discrepancies as they appear.**

The importance of these efforts extends beyond ensuring customers find accurate information. In *The Art of SEO*, experts Eric Enge, Stephan Spencer, and Jessie Stricchiola emphasize that consistency across citations is critical for building authority in search algorithms. When search engines encounter discrepancies, they may rank your business lower due to perceived unreliability. This can push you down in search results, directly impacting visibility and foot traffic.

Beyond fixing errors, proactive auditing uncovers opportunities to expand your presence. While reviewing your listings, consider platforms where your restaurant is not yet listed but should be. These could include niche food directories, local event sites, or even neighborhood blogs. Adding your restaurant to these platforms enhances your reach while strengthening your credibility in both the eyes of potential customers and search engines.

An effective audit process positions your restaurant for ongoing success. By ensuring your listings are accurate, managing changes promptly, and monitoring for consistency, you maintain not only a robust online presence but also the trust of those searching for their next meal.

Leveraging Aggregators for Widespread Visibility

"Did you know that a single aggregator like Yelp can influence up to 45% of a restaurant's search visibility?" Data aggregators have become the backbone of online business visibility, pulling together and distributing vital information to countless platforms. For restaurants, these aggregators aren't just tools; they are essential gateways for attracting local customers searching for dining options. Leveraging their reach effectively can ensure your restaurant not only gets found but also stands out.

At the heart of data aggregators lies their ability to centralize your business information. Platforms like Yelp, Foursquare, and Data Axle (formerly InfoGroup) collect details about your restaurant—name, address, phone number, hours, and more—and push it out to smaller directories, search engines, and GPS systems. When done correctly, this creates a ripple effect where your presence expands without requiring you to manage every listing manually. **Accuracy in your submissions to these aggregators is non-negotiable. A typo in your address or a wrong phone number can propagate across platforms, leading to frustrated customers and lower trust in your brand.**

Ensuring accurate data distribution begins with verifying what information aggregators already have about your restaurant. Tools like Moz Local and Yext allow you to audit your listings across major aggregators and pinpoint discrepancies. Once errors are identified, updating your data at the source becomes the critical step. By doing so, corrections will cascade to all connected platforms, creating uniformity and preventing conflicts between directories. **Think of this as setting the record straight: search engines value consistency, and a single, verified source of truth can boost your restaurant's rankings in local searches.**

Enhanced listings are another powerful feature of aggregators that often go underutilized. Many platforms allow restaurants to go beyond basic contact details by adding elements like menus, photos, special promotions, and links to online reservations. These details not only improve user experience but also make your listing more dynamic and appealing. For example, a well-crafted menu uploaded to Yelp can attract diners who might otherwise skip over a generic listing. **Platforms with rich content tend to perform better in search results because they answer more of the questions users are asking—What does this restaurant serve? Are there vegetarian options? Can I make a reservation now?**

The benefits of leveraging aggregators don't stop at visibility. They also provide invaluable insights into how customers are interacting with your business. Yelp, for example, offers analytics showing how often your listing is viewed and what actions customers are taking, such as clicking for directions or making a call. These insights can inform not only your digital strategy but also broader decisions about menu offerings or operating hours. **When you use data aggregators to their fullest potential, they become more than directories—they become tools for strategic growth.**

Maintaining this system requires vigilance. As your restaurant evolves, so should the information on your aggregator listings. New offerings, updated hours, or changes in contact details must be reflected quickly to avoid misinformation spreading across platforms. Routine audits ensure that your listings remain accurate and that any aggregator failures, such as outdated data persisting in smaller directories, are swiftly addressed.

Aggregators hold immense potential for any restaurant that aims to expand its online reach. By carefully managing how your data flows through these platforms, enhancing listings to showcase your unique offerings, and using the resulting insights, your restaurant can transform its digital presence into a competitive advantage. The visibility and credibility gained through these tools can help secure your spot as a trusted choice for local diners.

CHAPTER 5
COLLECTING AND MANAGING ONLINE REVIEWS
BOOST YOUR RESTAURANT'S REPUTATION WITH STELLAR REVIEWS

"What do people really think about your restaurant?" This question may seem simple, but the answer holds incredible power in shaping the future of your business. Online reviews are no longer just casual opinions; they are influential pieces of your reputation, guiding potential diners in deciding whether to step into your restaurant or move on to the next option. A study by BrightLocal revealed that 84% of consumers trust online reviews as much as personal recommendations, underscoring just how critical they have become in the dining industry.

Reviews are more than ratings—they are stories about customer experiences. Each one, whether glowing praise or constructive criticism, serves as a digital word-of-mouth recommendation. When managed well, they create a sense of trust and credibility, painting a picture of what people can expect when they visit your restaurant. But managing reviews involves more than simply hoping for five stars to appear. **It requires a structured approach to encourage posi-**

tive feedback while addressing challenges that might lead to negative reviews.

The process begins with making it easy for diners to leave reviews. Platforms like Google, Yelp, and Facebook provide essential spaces for customers to share their experiences, but many diners won't think to post a review unless prompted. A gentle reminder, such as a QR code linking to your review pages or a polite mention during checkout, can significantly increase review volume. **The key is to provide convenient pathways that fit seamlessly into the customer's interaction with your restaurant.**

Handling reviews effectively also means responding promptly and professionally to the feedback you receive. Positive reviews offer an opportunity to express gratitude and build customer loyalty. For negative feedback, how you respond can make the difference between losing a customer for good and turning a bad experience into a lasting connection. Studies have shown that customers often change their minds about a business after receiving a thoughtful and apologetic response to a poor review. **Acknowledging their concerns shows that you value their input and are committed to improvement.**

Another crucial aspect is monitoring reviews for trends. Frequent compliments about a specific dish can highlight a strong point in your menu, while recurring complaints about service can point to areas needing improvement. By paying close attention to patterns, you can address issues proactively and reinforce what you're already doing well. **Reviews become not just a tool for reputation management but also a source of valuable business insights.**

While reviews can sometimes feel beyond your control, there are strategies to influence them positively without resorting to shortcuts like fake reviews or bribery, which can damage credibility. Authenticity is what matters most, and consistently delivering great food, service, and ambiance will naturally encourage genuine praise.

Online reviews, when collected and managed strategically, serve as a bridge between your restaurant and potential customers. They amplify your best qualities, offer guidance for improvement, and, most importantly, build trust with your audience. As you approach the process of managing reviews, consider them not as a challenge but as an opportunity to highlight the soul of your restaurant and connect with the people who matter most: your diners.

> Using **DoSocialSmarter.com** ensures your restaurant maintains a stellar online reputation by streamlining the review process in a way that protects and enhances your brand. With its innovative system, **positive reviews (4 and 5 stars) are seamlessly directed to platforms like Google and Yelp**, boosting your visibility and credibility where it matters most. Meanwhile, reviews with 3 stars or less are intelligently filtered into private emails, allowing you to address concerns internally before they appear online. This approach not only helps resolve issues proactively but also demonstrates to customers that you care about their feedback and are committed to improvement. The result is a consistent flow of public praise paired with actionable insights, giving your restaurant the tools to grow its reputation while fostering trust and loyalty among your audience.

The Power of Reviews in Local SEO

It's hard to ignore the influence of reviews when a single

search can reveal hundreds of opinions about where to dine. Consider the case of a small pizzeria that climbed from obscurity to being the top-rated restaurant in its area. The owner, initially skeptical, began encouraging customers to leave reviews. Within months, the influx of glowing feedback not only boosted their online ranking but also doubled their reservations. This real-world impact highlights the critical role reviews play in shaping both visibility and trust.

Reviews are a cornerstone of local SEO, directly influencing how search engines rank businesses in local results. **Google's algorithms prioritize businesses with consistent, high-quality reviews, often ranking them above competitors with fewer or inconsistent feedback.** This is because reviews act as signals of relevance and reliability, reinforcing to search engines that your business delivers value to its customers. A strong collection of reviews can mean the difference between appearing on the coveted "local pack" or being buried beneath competitors.

Beyond rankings, star ratings play a crucial role in click-through rates. Studies have shown that **businesses with a 4-star rating or higher see significantly higher engagement rates compared to those with lower scores.** These ratings act as quick visual cues for potential customers, guiding their decision-making even before they click to learn more. For instance, a diner choosing between two restaurants on Google Maps is far more likely to opt for the one with a glowing 4.5-star rating and recent positive reviews than a competitor sitting at 3 stars with no recent feedback.

Reviews are also pivotal in driving conversions. Positive feedback from satisfied customers serves as social proof, reassuring potential patrons that your business delivers on its promises. **A collection of detailed reviews, particularly** those that mention specific dishes or exceptional service, creates a narrative that helps new customers visualize their own positive experience. A well-crafted review describing a perfect anniversary dinner or a delightful family outing can resonate more powerfully than any ad campaign.

Harnessing the power of reviews involves more than just collecting them; it's about maintaining quality and leveraging the insights they provide. Businesses that prioritize reviews not only build stronger connections with their audience but also position themselves for long-term success in an increasingly competitive digital landscape. The interplay between customer feedback and local SEO isn't just a trend—it's a fundamental strategy for growth.

Strategies for Encouraging Positive Reviews

Why do so many glowing reviews start with a phrase like, "They asked me how my meal was, and I just had to tell them"? This simple interaction reveals a key strategy: creating opportunities for customers to share their satisfaction. **Encouraging positive reviews isn't about luck; it's about cultivating the right moments and providing gentle guidance that feels natural and effortless.**

Ethical methods for requesting reviews start with genuine relationships. When staff members engage with customers, they should listen closely for signs of satisfaction. A warm comment about the food or an appreciative nod during service can be an opening to ask, "If you enjoyed your experience, we'd love it if you shared your thoughts online." **This type of invitation is respectful and rooted in the customer's own experience, making them more likely to follow through.** Avoid language that pressures or offers compensation for reviews, as most platforms, including Google and Yelp, strictly prohibit such practices.

Streamlining the process with tools can amplify these efforts. Automated review request systems simplify how businesses collect feedback without seeming impersonal. These tools often work through email or text, sending a friendly message shortly after a customer's visit. **Timing is crucial—requests sent within 24 hours of a positive experience are more likely to result in a review.** Advanced platforms can even segment audiences, tailoring the message tone and length to fit the customer's preferences. For instance, a quick, casual text might resonate with younger diners, while an email with a personalized thank-you could appeal to older patrons.

Incentives can also play a role, but they must align with platform guidelines. While direct rewards for reviews are not allowed, businesses can get creative with ways to encourage feedback. **A giveaway where participation involves leaving feedback—positive or constructive—can provide a fair and enticing opportunity.** For example, offering a chance to win a free meal or gift card demonstrates appreciation without tying the reward to the nature of the review.

Ultimately, successful strategies for encouraging positive reviews blend attentive service, well-timed requests, and thoughtful incentives. This approach ensures that feedback reflects the authentic experiences of satisfied customers while strengthening the business's reputation. When executed with care, these methods don't just boost review counts—they foster trust and build lasting connections with the community.

Handling Negative Feedback Like a Pro

"Reputation is what people say about you when you're not in the room," Jeff Bezos famously remarked. This wisdom rings true, especially when handling negative reviews. Every critical comment is more than a complaint—it's an opportunity to publicly demonstrate your professionalism, rebuild trust, and show customers you're listening.

The first step in responding to negative feedback is to stay calm and composed. A defensive or emotional response can escalate the situation, while a measured and thoughtful reply can turn things around. Begin by acknowledging the issue raised by the customer, even if their perspective seems exaggerated. A simple statement like, "Thank you for bringing this to our attention," shows that you value their input and sets a positive tone.

A professional response should also address the specific problem without assigning blame. Instead of focusing on what went wrong, emphasize what you're doing to make it right. For instance, if a customer mentions slow service, you could say, "We're sorry for the wait you experienced. We're reviewing our scheduling to ensure all guests are served promptly." This shows accountability while signaling improvement.

Thoughtful responses go beyond solving the immediate problem—they can showcase your business's values. Apologizing sincerely and explaining how you'll prevent similar issues can reassure not only the reviewer but also potential customers reading your reply. For example, a restaurant owner might write, "We strive to create a welcoming atmosphere for all our guests, and we're sorry we missed the mark during your visit. We're retraining our team to better meet your expectations."

Criticism often comes with a silver lining. It highlights

areas where your business can improve and offers insights you might otherwise miss. **Analyze patterns in negative feedback to identify recurring issues.** Is there consistent dissatisfaction with a specific dish, employee, or policy? Addressing these areas proactively can prevent future complaints and enhance the customer experience.

Real-life examples demonstrate how a well-crafted response can turn things around. When a customer left a review about an overcooked steak at a popular bistro, the owner responded by inviting them back for a complimentary meal and assuring them the kitchen had implemented stricter quality controls. Not only did the customer revise their review to reflect the positive resolution, but the thoughtful response also boosted the restaurant's image among readers.

Monitoring and responding to feedback isn't just about damage control—it's a chance to engage with your audience and build stronger relationships. When handled with care, even negative reviews can serve as a platform to highlight your business's commitment to excellence and accountability.

Showcasing Reviews Across Digital Channels

"There is no advertisement as powerful as a positive customer review," said Brian Solis, emphasizing the immense influence of testimonials in shaping public perception. Leveraging these endorsements effectively transforms them from static compliments into dynamic marketing assets that fuel credibility and conversions. The art lies in showcasing reviews across digital platforms in ways that amplify their impact and reach.

Embedding customer testimonials on your website anchors trust directly within your digital storefront. A dedicated review section—especially on landing pages or service pages—reinforces credibility at critical decision points. Highlighting recent, glowing feedback validates your business's quality and offers potential customers a glimpse into real experiences. For restaurants, adding star ratings or short quotes to your menu or homepage creates an inviting impression, signaling reliability and satisfaction.

Sharing reviews on social media provides a dual advantage. It not only keeps your content fresh and engaging but also positions your brand as one that values customer voices. Creative posts featuring positive feedback—formatted as visuals or accompanied by photos of the product or service mentioned—can spark conversations and generate shares. For example, a bakery might post a review about its "perfectly flaky croissants" alongside a photo of them fresh out of the oven. The personal touch makes the recommendation relatable and memorable.

Reviews can also be repurposed as testimonials in advertising campaigns, transforming kind words into conversion-driving tools. Including excerpts from customer reviews in email marketing or paid advertisements creates authenticity that is hard to replicate through traditional ad copy. Research supports this approach: according to BrightLocal's 2023 Consumer Review Survey, 49% of consumers trust reviews as much as personal recommendations, underscoring the value of incorporating these endorsements into broader marketing strategies.

Visual storytelling elevates the effectiveness of reviews as marketing assets. Video testimonials or short clips highlighting customer feedback can resonate deeply with audiences, adding a layer of emotion to the praise. A satisfied customer sharing their experience in their own words fosters a connection that written testimonials alone often cannot achieve.

Each review is more than feedback—it's an opportunity to showcase your brand's commitment to excellence. Thoughtfully displaying reviews across digital platforms integrates these authentic voices into your overall marketing strategy, reinforcing trust at every touchpoint. When handled with creativity and care, reviews become a lasting testament to the experiences your business delivers, ensuring they continue to inspire confidence and drive engagement.

CHAPTER 6
CRAFTING A CONTENT STRATEGY FOR LOCAL SEO
ENGAGE YOUR COMMUNITY WITH BLOG POSTS, MENUS, AND MORE

What makes a restaurant truly stand out in its community? More than just good food, it's often the stories, values, and personality behind the business that resonate most with diners. Crafting a content strategy designed for local SEO is the key to sharing these elements in a way that attracts attention and builds trust. From showcasing your menu to writing blog posts about local events, this approach allows you to connect meaningfully with your audience while improving your visibility online.

Effective content tailored for local SEO serves two primary purposes: engaging your community and increasing your chances of being discovered by new customers. Search engines reward businesses that offer valuable, localized content, making your efforts a win for both search rankings and customer relationships. A blog highlighting your chef's favorite seasonal ingredients, for example, not only humanizes your brand but also ensures your site is filled with fresh, relevant information that appeals to search algorithms.

Menus play a crucial role in this strategy, often serving as a diner's first impression of your restaurant. An optimized menu on your website, complete with descriptions, keywords, and high-quality images, does more than tempt potential guests—it helps your business rank higher when locals search for dishes you serve. Similarly, interactive content like event calendars or neighborhood guides positions your restaurant as an integral part of the community.

Storytelling is another powerful tool in this strategy. Sharing behind-the-scenes moments, staff profiles, or the origins of your recipes creates content that feels personal and engaging. Local diners are drawn to businesses that reflect their community's character, and your ability to tell these stories sets you apart from competitors.

This content strategy is not a one-size-fits-all approach. It requires careful planning and a deep understanding of what makes your audience tick. Each element, whether a blog post, a menu update, or a social media feature, must be purposeful and aligned with your broader goals of attracting local diners and building loyalty. By laying this foundation, you can create a lasting impact that draws in customers while enhancing your restaurant's online presence.

The Role of Content in Local SEO

How often do you search for a local restaurant, glance at its website, and immediately feel you've discovered the perfect spot? That immediate confidence is no accident—it's the result of intentional, well-crafted content. For restaurants, content isn't just about words on a page; it's the digital expression of their values, quality, and connection to the local community. More importantly, in the context of local SEO, content plays a pivotal role in building authority, engaging potential diners, and signaling relevance to search engines.

When a restaurant consistently produces valuable content, it establishes itself as a credible source within its market. Search engines prioritize websites that provide answers to user queries, and a rich blog post detailing the best wine pairings with seasonal dishes, for instance, can increase visibility while also demonstrating expertise. **Content that balances usefulness with creativity not only ranks better but also creates trust with visitors, which is essential for conversion.** This trust often translates into reservations, takeout orders, or visits from curious locals.

Restaurants are uniquely positioned to leverage a wide range of content types. Blogs can highlight recipes, local partnerships, or even the history of the neighborhood where the restaurant is located. Videos are particularly impactful, as they offer an engaging way to showcase cooking techniques, chef interviews, or behind-the-scenes glimpses of daily operations. Meanwhile, promoting local events—whether hosting a wine tasting or participating in a community festival—integrates the business into its surroundings and creates opportunities for organic engagement.

One successful example comes from a small family-owned pizzeria that began producing short weekly videos featuring the owner discussing different toppings and their origins. These videos not only attracted attention on social media but also improved the restaurant's local SEO rankings. By answering common questions like "What makes fresh mozzarella special?" the pizzeria tapped into search demand, driving more traffic to its website.

Local event promotion adds another layer of relevance. Announcing events through blogs or social media doesn't just bring in foot traffic; it also signals to search engines that the business is actively engaged with the local community. **Content connected to real-world events creates multiple touchpoints for customer engagement, whether through shares, likes, or direct participation.**

The value of content extends far beyond its immediate reach. Each piece of content—whether a blog, video, or event announcement—acts as a long-term asset. Optimized correctly, it continues to attract traffic long after its publication. For restaurants looking to stand out in a crowded local market, this compounding effect is invaluable, helping them remain top of mind with both loyal customers and new visitors. By committing to content that educates, entertains, and informs, restaurants can take control of their digital presence in a way that extends beyond traditional marketing efforts. High-quality content ensures the restaurant's story is told in a way that resonates with diners while simultaneously feeding the algorithms that determine search rankings. **For example, a well-written blog on sourcing local ingredients can serve as a resource for community members while strengthening SEO signals related to freshness and locality.**

It's not just about creating content for the sake of it—it's about crafting content with purpose. A restaurant's website becomes a central hub where menus, videos, blog posts, and event promotions work together to create a cohesive and engaging digital presence. This strategy isn't limited to large chains with extensive marketing budgets; small, independently-owned establishments can achieve significant results with thoughtful planning and consistency.

Ultimately, the role of content in local SEO is both

strategic and relational. It's the bridge between what customers seek online and the experiences they'll find in-person. Restaurants that master this dynamic not only increase their online visibility but also cultivate a loyal, engaged audience that keeps coming back for more. Whether through storytelling, resourceful content, or strategic event promotion, the possibilities are as varied as the dishes on the menu.

Creating Content That Ranks Locally

Why do some local businesses dominate search engine results while others remain buried beneath their competitors? One critical factor is how effectively they create content targeting local keywords. For restaurants, this can mean the difference between being the go-to spot for a "vegan-friendly café in Chicago" or fading into obscurity online. Strategic content creation is the key to ensuring your business connects with local customers, driving both traffic and engagement.

Writing blog posts targeting local keywords begins with understanding the language your community uses to search for places to eat. Tools like Google Keyword Planner or Uber-suggest can uncover phrases that locals frequently search for, such as "best brunch near the riverwalk" or "family-friendly pizza in downtown." When these terms are woven naturally into well-written blog posts, they enhance your website's relevance for those searches. But it's not just about throwing keywords onto a page—blog content should add value by answering common questions, telling stories, or showcasing what makes your restaurant special. For example, a blog post about the origin of your signature dish or your commitment to sustainable practices can resonate with readers while boosting your SEO ranking.

Seasonal and event-driven content is another powerful tool in your content strategy. A restaurant can create posts centered around local events, such as festivals or sports games, by tying them back to their offerings. "What to Eat Before the Annual Jazz Festival" or "Best Snacks for Watching the Big Game at Home" are timely topics that engage readers and increase visibility during high-traffic periods. Seasonal posts—like "Top Cocktails for Summer Evenings on the Patio" or "Comfort Foods to Warm You Up This Winter"—tap into your customers' seasonal cravings while keeping your website fresh and relevant.

What sets high-performing content apart is its ability to connect emotionally, and **storytelling is a proven method for achieving this connection.** Stories make your restaurant memorable by humanizing your brand and offering readers a glimpse into the passion behind the food. A post about how your chef was inspired by a family recipe, or a profile on a local farmer who supplies your ingredients, creates a narrative that customers can relate to. Storytelling also builds loyalty; people love supporting businesses that feel authentic and deeply rooted in their community.

One small-town bakery provides an example of how effective storytelling can be. When the owners blogged about the grandmother whose cookie recipe inspired their best-selling dessert, the post was shared hundreds of times on social media, driving record traffic to their site. More importantly, it turned casual readers into loyal customers who felt connected to the story behind the business. The bakery wasn't just selling cookies anymore—it was sharing a piece of its history.

By weaving local keywords, seasonal relevance, and

compelling storytelling into your content strategy, you create an online presence that attracts customers while building trust and authority. Whether someone is searching for your restaurant or simply exploring dining options in your area, thoughtful content ensures they'll find not just a business, but a reason to choose you. **With every post, you're not just improving SEO; you're building a lasting relationship with your community.**

Promoting Your Content for Maximum Reach

How can a small-town café get its blog posts in front of thousands of local readers without spending a fortune? The answer lies in promoting content effectively across digital channels. A robust promotion strategy transforms even the most humble blog post into a powerful tool for engagement and growth. Whether it's sharing on social media, partnering with influencers, or leveraging email campaigns, the key is to align these tactics with your audience's habits and interests.

Social media is an obvious starting point, but it requires more than simply posting a link. The most successful businesses tailor their posts to each platform. A colorful Instagram carousel showcasing a blog about seasonal recipes will engage a visually-driven audience, while a Facebook post might highlight the community aspect of a local event your restaurant sponsors. Short-form video content, such as a chef discussing the inspiration behind a dish mentioned in the blog, adds an engaging layer of authenticity. Platforms like TikTok and Instagram favor creativity, and these spaces are ripe for introducing your content to new audiences. Use relevant hashtags, geotags, and partnerships with food bloggers to ensure your posts reach beyond your existing followers.

Collaborating with local influencers is another effective way to boost visibility. These partnerships don't have to be costly or complex. Influencers with small but engaged audiences are often willing to collaborate for free meals or discounts. For example, a local fitness trainer might share your blog about healthy menu options, tagging your restaurant to drive traffic to both your site and theirs. Building these relationships over time creates trust, ensuring your content is seen as credible and community-focused. Studies have shown that micro-influencers often achieve better engagement rates than large-scale influencers, making them an ideal choice for small businesses targeting local markets.

Email campaigns remain one of the most reliable ways to reach your audience. When done thoughtfully, they are a direct line to customers who already have an interest in what you offer. Segmentation plays a crucial role here. A campaign targeting families might highlight a blog post about kid-friendly meals, while a campaign for young professionals could focus on after-work happy hour specials. Including snippets of your content in the email with an invitation to "read more" ensures higher click-through rates without overwhelming the recipient. Consistent emails that combine helpful information with your latest updates reinforce your brand's value over time.

One restaurant owner found success by combining all three tactics into a seamless strategy. After publishing a blog about their locally sourced ingredients, they shared it on Instagram Stories, tagging their partnering farms. The farms reshared the content, expanding the post's reach to a new audience. Simultaneously, the restaurant collaborated with a local food blogger to create a post about their farm-to-table philosophy, which linked back to the blog. Finally, they sent an email to their subscriber list, featuring a coupon for anyone who mentioned the blog when visiting. The result was a measurable uptick in both website traffic and foot traffic within a week.

Promoting content across multiple channels amplifies its impact. It's not just about getting more eyes on your blog or video; it's about ensuring those eyes belong to the right people—your local audience, potential customers, and community supporters. Crafting a thoughtful strategy that combines social media, influencer partnerships, and email campaigns can elevate your content from a static post to a dynamic tool for growth and connection.

Evaluating Your Content's Performance

"Content without feedback is like a conversation with yourself," a digital strategist once observed. This idea underscores the critical role of evaluating performance in content strategy. You may create stunning blog posts and engaging videos, but without understanding how your audience interacts with them, you're only guessing at what works. Measuring performance provides clarity, enabling you to refine your approach and amplify results.

The first step in evaluating your content is using tools that track traffic and engagement. Platforms like Google Analytics reveal the pages drawing the most visitors, how long they stay, and what actions they take. A sudden spike in visits to a seasonal blog post may highlight the success of promoting it through local event hashtags or a targeted email campaign. Social media insights provide additional layers of information, such as which posts generated the most shares, comments, and clicks. For example, if an Instagram Reel showcasing a behind-the-scenes kitchen tour outperforms a static photo post, you'll know where to focus your creative efforts moving forward.

To analyze what resonates most, look beyond raw numbers and dig into behavioral trends. Content that keeps readers on your site for longer durations often signals deeper engagement. Are readers clicking on links within your blogs, or are they exiting after the first paragraph? Heatmaps and scroll-tracking tools can show how far visitors read before leaving. Reviews and direct feedback also reveal which topics strike a chord. For instance, a blog about wine pairings that sparks enthusiastic customer comments suggests interest in more content focused on beverages or dining tips.

Iteration is the final and most crucial step in turning evaluation into growth. Refining your strategy based on data ensures your future content aligns better with audience expectations. If you notice that blogs with local keywords like "best pizza in [your city]" outperform generic titles, consider adopting a hyper-local focus across your site. Similarly, if email campaigns promoting recipes consistently lead to increased traffic, explore ways to make these promotions a regular feature. Experiment with tweaks to your posting schedule, tone, or format and observe how these changes influence outcomes over time.

One restaurant found great success by iterating based on their blog's metrics. Initially, their content highlighted recipes and general cooking tips. However, their analysis revealed that blogs featuring interviews with local farmers consistently received more shares and engagement. This insight prompted them to pivot toward storytelling about their community connections, which not only boosted traffic but also strengthened their local brand identity.

Effective evaluation isn't just about identifying what works—it's about learning how to replicate and expand upon success. Each blog post, video, or email campaign becomes a building block in a data-informed strategy. By combining traffic analysis, audience behavior insights, and a commitment to iteration, your content can evolve into a powerful tool for sustained growth.

CHAPTER 7
DEVELOPING A LOCAL SEO ACTION PLAN

TURN STRATEGIES INTO SUCCESS WITH A CLEAR AND MEASURABLE PLAN

Why do some businesses thrive with online visibility while others fade into the background? The difference often lies in having a clear and measurable plan. Strategies without action are like seeds left in a packet—they hold potential but never take root. In the world of local SEO, success depends not just on understanding the tactics but on systematically putting them to work.

An effective local SEO action plan begins by turning broad goals into specific, actionable steps. The framework includes everything from identifying relevant keywords to enhancing your Google Business Profile and crafting engaging local content. Each task must be tied to a timeline, clear objectives, and measurable outcomes. This process transforms an overwhelming digital landscape into manageable priorities, guiding your business toward meaningful growth.

As you begin to develop your plan, the most important focus is aligning your online presence with the needs of your local community. This means understanding the questions your audience is asking and tailoring your content, tools, and services to provide clear answers. By mapping out these needs and organizing your efforts around them, you create a strategy that resonates with both people and search engines.

No successful plan works in isolation. Collaboration and consistent tracking are essential. Whether you're managing tasks within your team or partnering with local professionals, communication keeps everyone aligned. Simultaneously, monitoring progress ensures you remain adaptable, responding to shifts in search trends, seasonal demands, or unexpected competition.

Throughout this process, the end goal remains simple: turning insights into actions that directly impact your visibility and engagement. A structured approach ensures that every effort contributes to your broader success, creating momentum that builds over time. Each action strengthens your presence, helping your business not only connect with more customers but also maintain relevance in an ever-changing digital landscape.

Setting Goals for Your Local SEO Campaign

What defines success in a local SEO campaign? For a small Italian bistro in Portland, it wasn't just having a presence online—it was setting clear goals that transformed their digital strategy into measurable growth. By aiming to increase reservations by 25% over three months and prioritizing weekend promotions, they created focus and tracked every milestone along the way. This deliberate approach turned vague aspirations into tangible results.

Defining realistic objectives begins with understanding your business's unique needs. A restaurant aiming to attract tourists may prioritize appearing in "best places to eat" lists, while a family diner might focus on dominating search results for nearby neighborhoods. Each business's situation demands a tailored approach, ensuring the goals align with its customer base, offerings, and competitive landscape. Without this alignment, even the best SEO tactics risk falling short of their potential.

Prioritizing areas of focus is essential to making progress. It's tempting to want everything—more reviews, higher rankings, increased website visits—but spreading efforts too thin often dilutes the impact. Instead, choose one or two high-priority objectives that align closely with the restaurant's immediate challenges. For instance, if weekday traffic is slow, focus on strategies that drive lunchtime visits, such as promoting daily specials through localized ads and blogs.

Clear goals also demand measurable outcomes. Generic aims like "boosting visibility" may sound ambitious but lack the precision needed for execution. Instead, think in terms of specific, quantifiable targets—such as improving Google Business Profile click-through rates by 15% or earning 50 new reviews in a month. This clarity allows you to track progress, evaluate effectiveness, and adjust tactics in real-time.

Tools play a vital role in defining and measuring these outcomes. Analytics platforms like Google Analytics, SEMrush, or BrightLocal can uncover patterns in user behavior, highlight what's working, and reveal gaps in your strategy. For example, if website data shows visitors leaving the menu page quickly, it might point to slow load times or unappealing design. Addressing these findings directly ties your actions back to the original goal, keeping the campaign on track.

It's also important to revisit and refine your objectives regularly. A successful campaign is rarely static. Trends evolve, competitors adapt, and customer preferences shift. Periodically reassessing your goals ensures that your efforts remain relevant and continue to drive results. If, for instance, a summer goal of filling outdoor seating is achieved early, you can pivot toward promoting holiday reservations or group catering services.

The strength of any local SEO campaign lies in its foundation. Setting thoughtful, specific, and measurable goals isn't just an early step—it's the blueprint for everything else. It creates a shared vision, ensures resources are allocated wisely, and provides benchmarks that make success easy to recognize. As the Portland bistro discovered, starting with clear objectives allows a business to turn abstract aspirations into achievements, one milestone at a time.

Allocating Time and Resources Effectively

Can an effective local SEO strategy work within a tight budget? Many small businesses believe robust digital marketing requires extensive resources, but the truth is, success often comes from smart planning, not unlimited spending. A neighborhood café in Boston, for example, increased online visibility by 40% in six months with a limited budget by combining free tools and strategic outsourcing. This approach shows that thoughtful allocation of time and resources can yield remarkable results.

Managing SEO on a budget starts with identifying tools that offer maximum value for little to no cost. Platforms like Google Analytics and Google Search Console provide robust insights into website traffic, keyword performance, and audience behavior—all without a subscription fee. For keyword research, tools such as Ubersuggest or AnswerThePublic help uncover trends specific to your area, ensuring your content aligns with what locals are searching for. **Choosing free or low-cost tools that meet your immediate needs allows you to reserve your budget for tasks that require specialized expertise.**

Outsourcing selectively is another way to stretch limited resources. Not every task requires in-house expertise, and for many small businesses, hiring a freelancer or agency for specific projects can save both time and money. For instance, outsourcing technical SEO audits or professional content creation ensures those high-impact areas are handled efficiently while allowing you to focus on daily operations. **When outsourcing, prioritize professionals with local knowledge, as they can better tailor their strategies to your audience's preferences.** Websites like Upwork or Fiverr can connect you with skilled freelancers at various price points, providing flexibility based on your budget.

Scheduling regular maintenance tasks is key to ensuring consistent progress without overwhelming your team. A structured calendar helps break down SEO into manageable pieces, preventing the process from becoming daunting or disorganized. **For example, dedicating one day each week to reviewing and updating your Google Business Profile ensures your hours, photos, and reviews are accurate and appealing to searchers.** Monthly tasks might include refreshing key pages with seasonal content or analyzing performance metrics to adjust priorities. This approach allows you to maintain momentum without disrupting the flow of daily business activities.

Balancing time and resources also means being realistic

about your limits. Focus on high-return activities like local link-building or earning positive reviews, as these often deliver more measurable results than spreading efforts across too many areas. **For example, partnering with local organizations to sponsor community events not only generates backlinks but also builds goodwill and strengthens ties with your audience.** Similarly, investing in strategies that leverage existing content, such as repurposing blog posts into social media updates, saves time while expanding reach.

The key to effective resource allocation lies in understanding what's essential versus what's optional. By leveraging free tools, outsourcing strategically, and creating a consistent maintenance schedule, businesses can achieve strong results without overspending. Just as the Boston café discovered, success isn't always about having the most resources—it's about using them wisely and with purpose.

Tracking Progress and Adapting Your Strategy

"How do you know if your efforts are paying off?" This question puzzled a family-owned bakery that started its first local SEO campaign. They had invested weeks in optimizing their website, collecting reviews, and posting on social media but were unsure how to measure success. By monitoring key metrics and adjusting tactics based on what worked, they doubled their online orders in three months without increasing their marketing budget. Their experience underscores a vital lesson: tracking progress and adapting your strategy isn't just helpful—it's essential.

Regularly monitoring rankings, website traffic, and customer reviews reveals what's working and what needs improvement. Tools like Google Analytics and Google Search

Console offer detailed insights into how people find your business online. For example, tracking keyword rankings over time helps determine whether your content is reaching the right audience. If a specific keyword starts to slip, you can revisit its related content to refresh or expand it. Reviews provide a different but equally important perspective. A surge in positive reviews could indicate that recent efforts to improve service or ask customers for feedback are succeeding. On the other hand, negative reviews might point to issues that need immediate attention.

Adjusting your tactics based on performance data ensures your resources are spent wisely. If a local blog post about seasonal menu items drives more traffic than general content, it's a clear sign to prioritize similar topics. For instance, one café discovered that posts highlighting local ingredients generated more engagement than other updates. They adjusted their strategy to focus on partnerships with nearby farmers and gained a loyal audience who appreciated the personal touch. Reallocating time and effort toward these high-performing areas ensures sustained growth without unnecessary effort.

Celebrating wins—both big and small—can keep your team motivated and focused. Reaching the first page of search results for a competitive keyword, receiving a record number of positive reviews, or surpassing a monthly traffic goal are all moments worth acknowledging. Publicly sharing milestones with your team fosters pride and strengthens commitment to the strategy. For example, a restaurant in San Diego regularly shared its SEO achievements during team meetings, which helped staff see how their contributions, like offering great service that earned glowing reviews, impacted the business's online visibility.

Keeping a pulse on progress also requires scheduling time for reflection and refinement. Regular intervals—monthly or quarterly—allow you to step back and assess the big picture. **Create a habit of comparing initial goals with current outcomes to identify gaps or unexpected successes.** This reflection ensures your strategy remains flexible and aligned with both market conditions and business objectives. Businesses that adapt to changes, such as shifts in customer preferences or new competitors, consistently outpace those that stick rigidly to their original plans.

Measuring progress is about more than numbers; it's about understanding how those numbers translate to real-world impact. A spike in traffic without an increase in orders might mean your content attracts browsers but not buyers, signaling a need to refine messaging or calls to action. Conversely, a modest increase in visitors paired with a rise in conversions could indicate quality over quantity in your outreach efforts. Always interpret metrics within the context of your unique goals and customer base.

An adaptable strategy, informed by clear metrics, is the key to long-term success. Businesses that regularly assess their progress, learn from their data, and celebrate their victories stay motivated and prepared to meet new challenges. Like the bakery that transformed its online presence, any business can achieve meaningful results by staying informed and agile.

Maintaining Long-Term Local SEO Success

"Success in SEO is a marathon, not a sprint," remarked a marketing consultant during a workshop on digital strategy. This statement resonated deeply with a small-town restaurant owner who had recently seen promising results from local SEO. Yet, as trends shifted and competitors emerged, the owner realized that maintaining those results required ongoing effort. This scenario captures an essential truth about SEO: consistency and adaptability are the lifelines of long-term success.

Ongoing optimization ensures your online presence remains competitive and relevant. Search engines like Google constantly update their algorithms to improve user experience. What worked six months ago may no longer yield the same results today. Regularly revisiting key elements such as keywords, meta descriptions, and on-page content is crucial to staying aligned with these changes. For example, if local search terms in your industry begin to reflect seasonal trends or emerging products, updating your content to incorporate those shifts can help sustain traffic and visibility.

Staying informed about local SEO trends equips you to act quickly and effectively. Tools like Google's updates blog, industry newsletters, and forums offer insights into the latest developments. For instance, the introduction of features like Google Posts or new review filters can significantly impact how customers interact with your business online. Embracing these updates early not only improves your rankings but also reinforces your reputation as a responsive and customer-centric brand.

As your business grows, your SEO strategies should evolve alongside it. A restaurant that begins with a focus on a single neighborhood may expand to multiple locations or diversify its menu. Each growth stage presents new opportunities and challenges for SEO. Expanding your strategy might involve targeting additional geographic keywords, creating landing pages for new services, or strengthening partnerships with local organizations to build backlinks. This proactive approach ensures that your online presence keeps pace with your physical expansion.

Scheduling periodic reviews of your progress helps maintain focus and alignment. Monthly or quarterly evaluations can uncover trends that might otherwise go unnoticed. For example, if data shows a consistent increase in mobile traffic, optimizing your site for mobile users should become a priority. Similarly, if reviews highlight a specific product or service as a standout, creating content around that success can amplify its reach.

Celebrating achievements, even small ones, fosters a sense of accomplishment and motivates continued effort. Acknowledging milestones, such as reaching a high review score or increasing traffic from a key demographic, reminds your team that their hard work is paying off. Sharing these wins internally or with loyal customers reinforces a positive feedback loop, inspiring everyone involved to maintain high standards.

Long-term success in local SEO is not just about maintaining what works; it's about anticipating what's next. Businesses that commit to continual improvement, stay informed about changes, and adapt their strategies to growth will find themselves well-positioned in an ever-changing digital landscape. Each adjustment, review, and celebration reinforces the foundation for sustainable visibility and ongoing connection with your local audience.

CONCLUSION

————

Turn casual diners into loyal fans with Do Social Smarter's proven system to grow your customer base, boost reviews, and drive foot traffic effortlessly.

Visit DoSocialSmarter.com today and discover how to keep your seats full and your competition behind.

DO SOCIAL SMARTER, LLC

marketing   est. 2017

BONUS: THREE CHAPTERS FROM "HOW TO HOST TRIVIA NIGHT"

Ready to Boost Your Slow Weekday Nights?

How to Host Trivia Night: Boost Your Bar's Revenue with Engaging and Memorable Trivia Events

UNLOCKING THE TRIVIA NIGHT PHENOMENON

Understanding the Appeal of Trivia Nights

Understanding the appeal of trivia nights, it's like stumbling upon a secret recipe. One that infuses a dull weekday evening with the zest of competition, the sizzle of social interaction, and the sweet aroma of learning, all while enhancing your business.

Let's take a moment to step into the shoes of trivia night regulars. Picture this - they've spent the whole day immersed in routine tasks. They're looking for an escape, a break from the monotony. They're not just seeking food and drinks; they're yearning for an experience, a memory to cherish. Trivia nights cater to this yearning, turning a mundane mid-week night into an unforgettable experience.

On the surface, trivia nights might seem like just a game, a handful of questions thrown at eager participants. But delve deeper, and you realize that it's much more than that. It's a social catalyst, transforming strangers into teammates, fostering bonds over shared laughter and collective triumphs. It offers the thrill of a healthy competition, that joyous rush when you recall an obscure fact from the depths of your memory. And the best part? This entire experience unfolds in the welcoming ambiance of your restaurant or bar, turning a one-time customer into a loyal patron.

• • •

Let's consider the time-honored British pub chain, Wetherspoons. Founded in 1979, Wetherspoons has earned a reputation for its warm, inviting atmosphere and value-for-money offerings. However, what truly sets it apart is its unique emphasis on community-building events, with trivia nights playing a leading role. It's not just about the revenues from the drinks and meals sold during these events; it's about cultivating a sense of community, transforming a public house into a "public home." Wetherspoons' success story illustrates the latent potential of trivia nights in attracting and retaining customers.

A trivia night is like a stage where every participant gets a moment in the spotlight, a chance to showcase their knowledge. It's a medium that taps into our innate curiosity, the childlike delight in learning something new. And this appeal cuts across demographics - young and old, students and professionals, locals, and tourists. The wide-ranging appeal of trivia nights ensures a diverse crowd, enhancing the vibrancy and dynamism of your establishment.

And then there's the learning aspect. It's a common misconception that learning is limited to classrooms and textbooks. Trivia nights dispel this notion, showing that learning can be fun, exciting, and social. Whether it's a quirky fact about a movie, an insightful piece of history, or a fascinating scientific concept, trivia nights feed the intellectual appetite of participants. It provides knowledge, served not with the rigidity of a lecture, but with the spontaneity of a conversation.

Richard Branson, the renowned founder of the Virgin Group, once said, "Fun is one of the most important - and underrated - ingredients in any successful venture." Trivia nights embody this spirit, infusing fun into your establishment's routine offerings. The laughter, the suspense, the cheers, they all add up to create an enchanting atmosphere, one that keeps your customers coming back for more.

The appeal of trivia nights lies not just in the immediate revenues from food and drink sales. It's about the long-term benefits - customer loyalty, word-of-mouth publicity, and a strong sense of community. These are the intangibles, the secret ingredients that transform a successful evening into a thriving business.

And so, as we grasp the essence of trivia nights, we realize it's not merely about asking questions and giving answers. It's about creating experiences, fostering connections, and celebrating knowledge. Trivia nights offer an avenue for patrons to enjoy, interact, and learn, all within the welcoming confines of your establishment. It's about understanding that in the business of hospitality, it's the experiences, more than the transactions, that make all the difference.

A true understanding of the appeal of trivia nights equips you with a powerful tool, one that can transform your business by turning a casual visitor into a devoted patron, a silent observer into an active participant, and a mundane evening into an engaging event. It's this understanding that gives you the edge, the ability to offer more than just food and drinks. It enables you to offer memories, experiences, and a vibrant community.

Assessing the Potential Revenue Increase

Assessing the potential revenue increase, it's like peering into a crystal ball to foresee a brighter, more prosperous future for your bar or restaurant. And who wouldn't want to predict and prepare for success? Especially when it's made possible by the humble yet potent concept of trivia nights.

Imagine the difference it would make, turning a slow, idle Tuesday evening into a bustling night brimming with energy and potential profits. The magical transformation trivia nights can bring to your earnings is like adding a vital ingredient to a recipe, turning it from ordinary to extraordinary.

For the sake of our conversation, let's construct an invisible bar graph, one that towers higher as we add the elements of a trivia night. Picture the income from your typical weeknight — a solid foundation, but with room for growth. Now imagine layering on the extra revenue from increased footfall on trivia nights — a significant boost, surely. Consider the drinks ordered as teams gather to strategize and the meals requested as they celebrate victories or console over losses. Bit by bit, your imaginary bar graph grows taller.

But the potential revenue increase isn't limited to the night of the event. Think of the conversations sparked, the memories created, and the stories shared the day after a trivia night. Patrons will come back, bringing friends, family, or colleagues, drawn by the allure of an engaging evening out. As word spreads, your establishment may become the go-to place for trivia enthusiasts, a title that comes with a loyal and expanding customer base.

In the world of business, there's a well-known saying by Robert Kiyosaki, author of the best-seller "Rich Dad Poor Dad" — "The most successful people are mavericks who aren't afraid to ask 'why'?" Why can't a weeknight earn as much as a weekend? Why can't a bar or a restaurant be a place not just for food and drink, but also for entertainment and learning? By hosting trivia nights, you're challenging the status quo, and this innovative approach is bound to reflect positively on your revenues.

Yet, assessing potential revenue increase is more than just tallying up the extra orders. It's about seeing the bigger picture. Trivia nights contribute to a vibrant and inviting atmosphere that strengthens your brand image. This elevated image can help you stand out in a competitive market, allowing you to command higher prices without alienating your customer base.

But of course, all this isn't to say that running trivia nights is a guaranteed golden goose. Like any business initiative, it requires careful planning, execution, and adjustment. What works for one establishment might not work for another. Factors such as location, customer demographics, and local competition all come into play. It's crucial to adopt a balanced view, seeing trivia nights not as an instant cash grab but as a strategic investment in building a stronger, more dynamic business.

In this light, assessing the potential revenue increase from trivia nights is akin to drafting a roadmap to your business's future growth. It's about understanding how this simple, yet powerful initiative can lead to broader, lasting benefits — increased footfall, customer loyalty, positive word-of-mouth, and an enhanced brand image. And once these benefits translate into financial terms, you may just find that your business is not just surviving, but thriving.

The potential of trivia nights is vast and varied. It's an innovative approach to enhancing both customer experience and your bottom line. By diving into this exciting endeavor, you're not just betting on a single night's profit, but investing in a more vibrant and profitable future. So, as we chart the growth of your business, remember — it's not just about the extra income from one night, but the ripple effect it can create, boosting revenues, one trivia question at a time.

Identifying the Ideal Customer for Trivia Nights

Identifying the ideal customer for trivia nights is like unearthing the hidden treasure key to unlocking the door of prosperity for your bar or restaurant. A successful business knows its customers, their likes, dislikes, habits, and motivations. Understanding your trivia night audience can guide you to tailor your events, crafting experiences that resonate with them, lure them in, and keep them coming back for more.

Paint a mental picture of your ideal trivia night participant. They are not just customers who buy a round of drinks and a plate of appetizers. They are engaged, they participate, they bring their friends, they come back week after week. They transform a simple transaction into a thriving community, turning your bar or restaurant into a buzzing hive of activity and camaraderie.

Think of the groups you see huddled together at your establishment, and in similar establishments around town. Students seeking a break from their academic rigors, young professionals eager for a fun wind-down from work, enthusiasts looking for a challenge, and friends searching for an alternative to their usual hangouts. Trivia nights can cater to all these demographics, and more. The beauty of trivia lies in its universal appeal – it cuts across age, profession, and even cultural boundaries.

In his book "Start With Why," author Simon Sinek writes, "People don't buy WHAT you do; they buy WHY you do it." The same applies to your trivia night audience. They are there not just for the questions and answers. They are there for the experience, the thrill of competition, the joy of learning, the bond of teamwork, and the unique atmosphere you provide.

Knowing this, your ideal customer is one who values these experiences. They enjoy the thrill of a challenge, the cama-raderie of teamwork, and the joy of learning. They appreciate a well-run event that starts on time, maintains a brisk pace, and ends leaving them wanting more.

Equally important to identifying your ideal customer is understanding how to attract and retain them. No matter how well you know your audience, if they don't know about your trivia nights, or if they don't enjoy them, they won't come, and they certainly won't come back.

Promotion, then, is as crucial as identification. Use channels your audience frequents — social media, local listings, in-house advertisements — to let them know about your trivia nights. Word-of-mouth is another powerful tool. An enthused customer can become a voluntary ambassador, bringing in more like-minded patrons.

What keeps them coming back is the quality of the trivia night itself. The questions should be interesting, challenging but not too difficult, broad-ranging but not too obscure. The pace should be brisk but not hurried, the atmosphere energetic but not chaotic. And remember, it's not just about the trivia; it's about the overall experience. Friendly service, good food and drink, and a comfortable environment all contribute to making your trivia night an event to look forward to.

Understanding your customers' expectations and experiences can guide you in tailoring your trivia nights, ensuring they meet, and hopefully exceed, these expectations. It also helps you identify potential improvements, innovations, and opportunities for growth.

Identifying the ideal customer for trivia nights, then, is not just about knowing who they are, but understanding why they come, what they enjoy, how to attract them, and how to keep them coming back. It's about recognizing the role trivia nights play in their lives and in the community at large. It's about aligning your business goals with their desires and expectations, creating a symbiotic relationship where everyone wins.

• • •

In the end, the key to unlocking the treasure of your business potential lies not in a single ideal customer but in the vibrant, diverse community of trivia lovers who frequent your establishment. As they find joy, camaraderie, and challenge within your walls, you'll find business growth, customer loyalty, and the satisfaction of providing a valued service to your community. The treasure, it seems, isn't hidden after all. It's there every trivia night, in the form of your engaged, enthusiastic customers, waiting to be recognized, appreciated, and served.

Understanding the Appeal of Trivia Nights:

- Trivia nights transform mundane evenings into memorable experiences.
- Trivia nights foster social interaction, teamwork, and competition.
- Trivia appeals to a wide range of demographics, enhancing the vibrancy of your establishment.
- Trivia nights provide a fun and social way to learn new things.
- Trivia nights contribute to customer loyalty, word-of-mouth publicity, and a sense of community.
- Trivia nights offer more than just food and drinks, providing engaging experiences and lasting memories.

Assessing the Potential Revenue Increase:

- Trivia nights can significantly boost revenue on weeknights.
- Extra orders during trivia nights contribute to increased profitability.
- Trivia nights can attract new customers and encourage repeat visits.

- Trivia nights contribute to a vibrant atmosphere, enhancing brand image.
- Trivia nights can lead to higher prices without alienating customers.
- Trivia nights require careful planning and execution for long-term success.

Identifying the Ideal Customer for Trivia Nights:

- Identify customers who value the experience, competition, and learning opportunities of trivia nights.
- Understand the demographics and motivations of your ideal trivia night participants.
- Use targeted promotion channels to attract your ideal customers.
- Maintain a high-quality trivia night experience to retain customers.
- Continuously understand and meet customer expectations to enhance the trivia night experience.
- Recognize the role of trivia nights in the lives of customers and the community.
- Cultivate a symbiotic relationship with trivia lovers for business growth and customer satisfaction.

CRAFTING IRRESISTIBLE TRIVIA QUESTIONS

Assembling Diverse Topics

Assembling diverse topics for your trivia night is like concocting a tantalizing recipe that leaves everyone salivating for more. The beauty of trivia is that it doesn't discriminate — everyone from science nerds to history buffs, from sports fans to movie enthusiasts, can find their niche. Your challenge, then, is to find a balance, a blend of topics that engages your audience and keeps them guessing.

Picture a vibrant trivia night scene. The atmosphere is electric, the stakes are high, and every participant is waiting with bated breath for the next question. Suddenly, a question about the quantum physics concept of superposition is thrown into the mix. A few people jump in excitement, but most are left scratching their heads. And therein lies your first lesson: balance is key.

You want to ensure that your questions span a broad spectrum, from pop culture to geography, from sports to science, from history to current events. The goal is not to stump participants with overly specialized or obscure questions, but to offer something for everyone, making sure that each person in the room feels challenged, yet able to contribute.

· · ·

Diversity in your question set also helps maintain the interest and energy levels in the room. Imagine a sequence of questions solely about World War II. After the initial excitement, interest might dwindle and the energy could sag. However, by interspersing those war questions with queries about, say, the latest Marvel movie, the origin of the Margherita pizza, or even quirky international customs, you can hold onto that energy and interest.

Consider also the varying degrees of difficulty within each topic. Not all sports questions have to be about obscure statistics, not all history questions need to be about ancient civilizations. Mix it up with easy, medium, and hard questions. For example, alongside a question about the details of the Treaty of Versailles, include a simpler one about the country from which pizza originated. This ensures that beginners don't feel overwhelmed and trivia veterans don't get bored.

In his 2002 book, "The Tipping Point," author Malcolm Gladwell talks about the concept of 'stickiness' — certain specific content makes the message memorable. This 'stickiness' is what you're aiming for in your trivia night questions. You want people to leave at the end of the night, not just entertained and educated, but with questions that stick in their minds and bring them back next week.

One proven method to achieve this is by relating your questions to popular and relatable themes. For example, if a major sporting event, like the Super Bowl, is around the corner, include some questions about it. If a blockbuster movie is being released, add a few questions about the franchise. This not only makes your trivia night timely and relevant but also adds a sense of familiarity and relatability.

Also, don't underestimate the power of a well-placed quirky or humorous question to lighten the mood and add a dash of unpredictability. Who wouldn't remember a question about the national animal of Scotland (it's the unicorn!) or the law against tying a giraffe to a telephone pole in Atlanta?

Assembling diverse topics, then, isn't just about quantity, it's about quality, balance, and timing. It's about understanding your audience, reading the room, and adjusting on the go. It's about making the trivia night not just a quiz, but a fun, engaging, and memorable experience.

At the heart of it all, your trivia night should be a reflection of our wonderfully diverse world — a world full of facts, stories, and knowledge, waiting to be explored and shared. So go ahead, mix and match, and create a trivia night as diverse, dynamic, and vibrant as the world itself. It's not just about winning or losing, it's about learning, laughing, and connecting. And who knows, while helping others learn, you might just learn something new yourself.

Structuring Questions for Maximum Engagement

. . .

Unlocking the secret to structuring questions for maximum engagement is like discovering the ultimate spice mix that transforms a simple dish into a crowd favorite. When you master this art, you get the magic key to hosting trivia nights that buzz with excitement, attracting new patrons and retaining old ones, boosting your bar and restaurant revenue.

Every question at your trivia night is an opportunity to stoke the flames of curiosity, competition, and camaraderie. A well-structured question, much like a well-crafted story, has the power to captivate an audience, keep them on their toes, and leave them eager for more. But how do you create such questions?

Let's start by thinking about the different types of questions. We usually think of questions as being either easy or hard, but consider another dimension: open-ended versus closed-ended. Closed-ended questions have a single, definitive answer. They're great for competition, for separating the trivia champs from the chumps. But don't overlook the power of open-ended questions, ones that invite debate and discussion. These questions can ignite the kind of passionate debates that make trivia nights so much fun.

For example, instead of asking, "Who won the 2020 Best Actor Oscar?" you could ask, "Who should have won the 2020 Best Actor Oscar and why?" This sparks conversation, gives everyone a chance to share their opinion, and keeps the night lively and engaging. Remember, trivia nights aren't just about what people know, but also about what they think, feel, and believe.

Now, let's talk about difficulty. A mix of easy, medium, and hard questions is crucial to maintain interest. Easy questions make participants feel good, give them a confidence boost. Medium questions provide a bit of challenge, but still within reach. Hard questions separate the trivia regulars from the newbies. But there's a fourth type of question, one that can be a game-changer: the seemingly easy question with a twist.

For instance, you might ask, "What's the capital of Australia?" Most people would quickly answer "Sydney" or "Melbourne", but the correct answer is "Canberra." These kinds of questions add a dash of unpredictability, keep people on their toes, and inject some fun into the proceedings.

Of course, a well-structured question isn't just about the content. It's also about the delivery. A touch of drama, a pause at the right moment, a teasing hint — these can transform a regular question into a thrilling one. Imagine asking a question about the highest-grossing movie of all time. You could simply ask it straight, or you could build it up, talk about the enormous sums of money involved, throw in some red herrings, and then hit them with the question. Which approach do you think would be more engaging?

· · ·

Finally, always remember the golden rule of trivia nights: they're meant to be fun. Don't get so caught up in crafting perfect questions that you forget to make them enjoyable. Throw in some silly questions, some absurd ones, even some ridiculous ones. Keep them laughing, keep them entertained, and they'll keep coming back.

Mastering the art of question structuring is not a one-night affair. It requires practice, intuition, and a keen understanding of your audience. But once you get the hang of it, you'll see your trivia nights transform. The energy levels will soar, the laughter will ring louder, the discussions will become more animated, and before you know it, you'll be running the most sought-after trivia nights in town. And isn't that the goal? To create an experience that people look forward to, week after week. It's more than just a trivia night. It's a community, a tradition, a highlight in people's social calendars. And with well-structured questions, you can make it all that and more.

Balancing Difficulty Levels for Broad Appeal

Balancing difficulty levels for broad appeal in trivia nights is like a chef preparing a multi-course meal that caters to different taste preferences. A bit of sweet, a dash of spice, a touch of tangy - all these blend together to create a flavor profile that satisfies everyone. In the same way, a trivia night that incorporates varying difficulty levels can attract a diverse crowd, enhancing the vibe and boosting the revenue of your bar or restaurant.

Trivia nights have an undeniable charm. The anticipation of each question, the thrill of competition, the joy of knowing obscure facts – all these elements blend together to create a captivating environment. But it's the variety of questions that's the secret sauce in this recipe, which keeps participants engaged and coming back for more.

Imagine you have a crowd of mixed trivia aficionados, from green beginners to seasoned pros. If you pepper the night with only difficult questions, you risk making it too challenging for novices, resulting in frustration. If you stick to easy questions, your trivia veterans might lose interest. This is where the balance comes in.

Having a wide range of questions can accommodate all your participants. The easy questions help beginners gain confidence, while the hard ones challenge the experts and keep them engaged. A trivia night isn't merely about winning; it's about participating, learning, and most importantly, having fun.

As a trivia host, you're like a tour guide on a voyage of discovery. Each question should take your participants on a mini adventure, unlocking bits of knowledge, stirring their curiosity. For this, you need to focus not only on the content of the questions but also on their format and delivery. A hard question isn't necessarily one with a tough answer; it could be an easy answer concealed in a cleverly phrased question. Similarly, an easy question isn't just about basic facts; it could be a common knowledge presented with a unique twist.

Now, you might be thinking, how does one decide the difficulty level of a question? Well, it's not an exact science. It's about understanding your audience, knowing what they might find easy or difficult. Keeping a pulse on the interests, backgrounds, and general knowledge levels of your crowd is key. You'll learn this over time, by observing, interacting, and listening to your crowd.

Remember, variety is the spice of life, and the same holds true for trivia nights. Blend in some questions about history, pop culture, sports, science, and more. Just as in a delightful meal, where you experience different tastes and textures, a trivia night should offer a smorgasbord of questions that appeal to everyone.

Let's not forget, the ultimate aim is to create a lively, fun-filled atmosphere that keeps people coming back. A well-balanced trivia night can turn into a social highlight, a place where friendships are forged, a space that provides a break from the mundane, and an opportunity to learn and have fun.

• • •

So, embrace the role of the trivia chef. Experiment with your ingredients – the questions. Mix and match the difficulty levels. Observe your patrons – their expressions, their reactions. Refine your recipe as you go along. Soon, you'll have the perfect blend that keeps your bar buzzing with eager patrons, night after night. They'll come for the trivia, stay for the ambiance, and return for the experience. In the process, you'll have not just boosted your revenue, but also created a community, a destination, a memory. After all, isn't that the essence of a truly great trivia night?

Why Purchasing Premade Trivia Questions Can Ensure a Consistent and Quality Trivia Night

Investing in premade trivia questions is like having a treasure chest filled with gems of knowledge. With them, you can create consistently engaging trivia nights that boost your bar's appeal and revenue. Now, you may be wondering, why purchase premade trivia questions when you can craft your own? Well, let's explore that.

Picture this: You're hosting your first trivia night. You've gathered a bunch of questions, some from the internet, some you made up, and a few from that dusty old trivia game in the basement. The night kicks off, and soon, you find the crowd losing interest. The questions are either too easy, too hard, or just irrelevant. That's the equivalent of a chef throwing random ingredients into a pot and hoping for a culinary masterpiece. The result can be less than appetizing.

Contrast this with a trivia night based on professionally crafted questions. Every query is like a finely tuned note in a symphony, creating a harmonious blend of engagement, competition, and fun. These questions are designed with balance in mind, catering to different knowledge levels and interests. They are topical, relevant, and designed to intrigue, entertain, and challenge.

Premade trivia questions come from seasoned trivia masters who understand the craft. They know that the right question can spark lively debates, stimulate memories, and create unforgettable moments. They understand that a great trivia question isn't just about the fact it presents but how it's phrased, how it nudges participants to dig deep into their memory banks and pull out that nugget of knowledge they didn't even know they had.

Time is another significant factor. Creating high-quality trivia questions isn't a quick task. It involves research, verification of facts, and the careful phrasing of questions and answers. In a bustling bar or restaurant environment, this could mean hours of work that you could otherwise use to enhance your business in other ways. With premade trivia questions, you have more time to focus on creating the perfect atmosphere for your trivia night – planning the menu, arranging the seating, training your staff to handle the event, and promoting the night to draw in the crowd.

Another advantage of professionally made trivia questions is their versatility. Most providers offer a range of categories and difficulty levels, allowing you to customize the trivia experience for your crowd. It's like having a well-stocked pantry from which you can pick and choose the ingredients for a memorable trivia feast.

But let's get back to your business. A well-organized trivia night can do wonders for your establishment. It can transform a slow night into a bustling one, draw in new customers, and turn occasional visitors into regular patrons. It creates a sense of community, a vibrant atmosphere that people want to be a part of, and memorable experiences that keep them coming back.

At the end of the day, purchasing premade trivia questions is an investment in your business. It's a tool that can drive customer engagement, boost your revenue, and set your bar or restaurant apart in a competitive market. Just like a master chef relies on high-quality ingredients for their signature dishes, a top-notch trivia host relies on well-crafted questions for a successful trivia night.

And remember, trivia nights aren't just about quizzing people on random facts. They are about creating an atmosphere of camaraderie, sparking curiosity, and offering a fun and engaging escape from the daily grind. So why not give your trivia nights the professional touch they deserve?

It's time to raise the bar. *Visit cheaptriva.com, and let the professionals help you craft the perfect trivia night.* With compelling weekly trivia questions and free social media advertising support, you can create an event that resonates with your patrons and keeps them coming back for more. Step into the spotlight and let the trivia magic unfold.

Key Lessons

Assembling Diverse Topics:

- Find a balance of topics that engages your audience and caters to a wide range of interests.
- Include a variety of topics, such as pop culture, geography, sports, science, history, and current events.
- Avoid overly specialized or obscure questions to ensure inclusivity and participation.
- Intersperse questions from different topics to maintain interest and energy levels.
- Consider the timing and relevance of questions by incorporating popular and timely themes.
- Create questions that are memorable and spark conversations or debates.

Structuring Questions for Maximum Engagement:

- Balance closed-ended and open-ended questions to encourage participation and discussion.
- Vary the difficulty levels of questions, including easy, medium, hard, and seemingly easy questions with twists.

- Use delivery techniques, such as drama, pauses, and hints, to make questions more engaging.
- Focus on creating a fun and enjoyable trivia night experience.
- Craft questions that leave a lasting impact and make participants want to return.

Balancing Difficulty Levels for Broad Appeal:

- Include questions of varying difficulty levels to accommodate different knowledge levels.
- Offer a mix of easy, medium, hard, and seemingly easy questions with twists.
- Observe and understand your audience to determine appropriate difficulty levels.
- Blend questions from different topics to cater to a diverse crowd.
- Strive to create a lively, fun-filled atmosphere that keeps participants engaged.

Why Purchasing Premade Trivia Questions Can Ensure a Consistent and Quality Trivia Night:

- Premade trivia questions are designed by professionals with expertise in crafting engaging questions.

- Professionally crafted questions provide a balanced and well-structured trivia experience.
- They save time and effort compared to creating questions from scratch.
- Premade questions offer versatility, allowing customization based on categories and difficulty levels.
- Using high-quality trivia questions enhances the overall experience, attracts customers, and boosts revenue.
- Trivia nights can create a sense of community and memorable experiences that keep patrons coming back.

MASTERING THE ART OF TRIVIA NIGHT PLANNING

Setting the Perfect Date and Time

Finding the sweet spot in setting the perfect date and time for your bar or restaurant events can make the difference between a bustling night and empty seats. The secret to this success is understanding your clientele and their habits, and then aligning your events accordingly.

Consider the rhythm of the week. Most people unwind on weekends, and weekdays often hold potential for niche crowds. You might think, why not host an event every day? While enthusiasm is admirable, balance is key. Remember, the moon shines brightest on the darkest nights.

For instance, if you know your crowd is largely made up of working professionals, weekday afternoons might not be the best choice. They're likely caught up in the hustle and bustle of work. But what about Wednesdays? It's often dubbed as 'hump day,' the middle of the work week when people could use a bit of relaxation to reenergize for the rest of the week. How about transforming that into a lively trivia night?

Don't overlook the power of specific dates. National holidays, sports events, or local festivities can turn an ordinary day into an opportunity. This is the perfect time to weave in themes into your trivia night or create a special menu. It's a matter of finding harmony between the calendar and your creativity.

. . .

Now, about the time of day. The evening is often the preferred choice for many bar events. After a day's work, people are ready to unwind. But don't underestimate the potential of other time slots. Late afternoons can draw in the early bird crowd, while a late-night event can appeal to night owls.

Determining the perfect time also requires a good understanding of your event's nature. A sophisticated wine tasting might suit an early evening, while a rock-and-roll themed trivia night could fit perfectly into the late-night slot. The event should dictate the time, just as the melody guides the dance.

Of course, all this planning means little without effective communication. It's essential to keep your patrons in the loop. If people don't know about your event, they can't attend. In the age of social media, it's easy to get the word out. A well-placed post or tweet can reach hundreds, even thousands, of potential customers.

Remember, the goal is not just to fill seats, but to create a memorable experience that will keep your patrons coming back. It's not just about the here and now, but also about planting seeds for future success.

. . .

Every bar or restaurant has a personality, a unique rhythm that sets the beat for its success. Finding the right date and time for your events is about listening to that rhythm and harmonizing with your customer's needs and wants. It's a dance of numbers and intuition, logic and creativity. But when you get it right, it can turn an ordinary night into an unforgettable experience.

Take a moment to reflect on your establishment's unique rhythm. When do your customers come alive? When do they seek refuge in the comfort of your space? Finding the answers to these questions can guide you in setting the perfect date and time for your events. So listen to the beat, feel the pulse, and let the rhythm of your business lead the way. The dance floor is yours.

Organizing the Venue Layout

Organizing the venue layout is like conducting a symphony, where each element plays its part to create a harmonious experience. The importance of this task lies in its power to transform your venue into an enticing and functional space that can significantly boost your bar or restaurant's revenue.

Diving right in, the layout should mirror the rhythm and energy of the event you're hosting. Be it a laid-back trivia night or a buzzing happy hour, each corner of your venue plays a crucial role. It's not just about placing furniture, but also about creating spaces for experiences.

Imagine this: you have a trivia night scheduled. Your patrons will need tables to gather around, and a spot from where the host can interact with the audience. A focal point, let's say. The layout should facilitate this interaction, allowing every guest to feel included. A central spot for the host, surrounded by strategically placed tables, creates an intimate, shared experience. It's the power of design, turning a simple trivia night into a memorable event.

While organizing the layout, you must consider the natural flow of your venue. Your goal is to guide your guests effortlessly through the space. Your bar, seating area, restrooms - the placement of these elements should make sense. It's like plotting a map for an exciting adventure, where every stop is effortlessly linked to the next.

Now, let's not forget about the heartbeat of any bar or restaurant - the bar area. Position it to be easily accessible, yet not intrusive to the flow of your event. The bar is more than just a spot to grab drinks; it's a social hub, a meeting point. Its location should invite patrons to mingle and connect. The bar's placement is crucial, as it's the anchor that can set the mood for the entire evening.

· · ·

Seating arrangements should also be a priority. They should invite conversation and interaction, making the guests feel comfortable. The size of the tables, the distance between them, and their position in relation to the event's focal point - all of this matters. The goal is to create a setting that allows people to engage with the event and with each other, just like a perfect melody that brings people together.

The layout is not only about the guests but also about the team working behind the scenes. The staff should be able to move around smoothly, serve the guests efficiently, and manage the event without any hitches. It's about creating harmony between the visible and the invisible parts of your venue.

Remember, there is no one-size-fits-all when it comes to organizing the venue layout. Every space has its unique character, and every event has its own vibe. It's like a puzzle, with each piece fitting perfectly into the other, creating a complete picture.

So, think of your venue as a blank canvas, and the event as the artwork you want to create. The way you organize the layout can either make the colors pop or blend them into a blur. Consider the flow, the interactions, the comfort of your guests, and the efficiency of your staff. Once you've figured all this out, you can transform your venue into a stage set for unforgettable experiences.

· · ·

Mastering the art of organizing the venue layout can give your business the edge it needs. It's about blending aesthetics with functionality, and charm with efficiency. And when you get it right, your venue becomes more than just a space; it becomes a destination that leaves a lasting impression. So, embrace this challenge, conduct your symphony, and let the music play!

Designing the Ideal Trivia Night Schedule

Like a roller coaster, the perfect trivia night needs the right balance of exciting ups, calming downs, and heart-stopping moments to keep the riders - or in our case, the participants - engaged throughout the ride. Striking this balance can drastically boost the revenue and popularity of your bar or restaurant.

The heart of a trivia night lies in its schedule. You're not just setting a timetable, but also setting the rhythm of the night. Too short, and you may leave your patrons yearning for more without realizing the potential of your event. Too long, and you risk dampening the excitement and leading towards ennui. Much like watching a captivating movie or an intense sports match, the sweet spot for a trivia event tends to hover between one and a half to three hours.

· · ·

A well-thought-out trivia schedule starts with the simple act of understanding your audience. Who are they? What do they like? When are they the most energetic? Are they early birds or night owls? The answers to these questions can set the tone for your trivia night. For instance, if your patrons are energetic night owls, a later trivia schedule might be perfect. But if they're early birds, consider an after-work slot.

Don't forget the power of suspense and the art of pacing. Start with a bang to grab their attention. Then, slow down a little to give them a breather. Remember to build up towards an exciting climax. Just as a roller coaster starts with a thrilling ascent, followed by a series of twists and turns, and culminates in a thrilling finish, your trivia schedule should follow a similar pattern.

Imagine this: It's trivia night at your bar. The crowd is buzzing with anticipation. The game begins with an electrifying first round, fueling the energy in the room. Following this, a fun, interactive round allows participants to catch their breath, maybe grab another drink, while maintaining their interest. Then, the heat turns up with challenging rounds that test their trivia prowess, leading up to an exhilarating grand finale. Now, wouldn't that be a trivia night to remember?

Incorporating breaks is equally crucial. You don't want your patrons to feel overwhelmed. Strategically placed intermissions for drinks and food not only give them time to relax but also contribute to your revenue. These breaks can also be great opportunities for socializing and building a community around your trivia night.

A well-structured schedule isn't just for the participants. It also helps your team deliver a flawless experience. The bar staff can plan when they'll be busiest, the kitchen can predict food orders, and the host can maintain the pace of the evening.

It's like conducting an orchestra. Each musician knows when to play their part, resulting in a harmonious performance. A trivia night is no different. Each segment, each break, each question contributes to creating an experience that your patrons will love and remember.

However, remember that no two nights are the same. Be open to feedback, learn from each event, and adapt. The perfect trivia schedule today might need tweaking tomorrow, and that's okay. Stay flexible, stay aware, and most importantly, stay in tune with your audience.

So, set the rhythm, control the pace, and create suspense. Make your trivia night more than just a game. Make it an experience. Crafting the perfect trivia night schedule could be your ticket to a successful, profitable, and fun-filled evening at your bar or restaurant. Now, it's time to get started. It's time to design that roller coaster ride!

Key Lessons

Setting the Perfect Date and Time:

- Understanding your clientele and their habits is essential in selecting the ideal date and time for your events.
- Consider the rhythm of the week and find the balance between weekdays and weekends to attract different crowds.
- Take advantage of specific dates, holidays, sports events, or local festivities to create themed trivia nights or special menus.
- Choose the time of day that aligns with the nature of your event and consider the preferences and energy levels of your target audience.
- Effective communication and promotion through social media are crucial for ensuring that people know about your events.

Organizing the Venue Layout:

- The layout should reflect the energy and theme of the event, creating spaces that facilitate interaction and engagement.

- Consider the natural flow of the venue, ensuring that the placement of elements like the bar, seating areas, and restrooms makes sense and guides guests effortlessly through the space.
- The positioning of the bar should be easily accessible, inviting patrons to socialize and creating a central hub for the event.
- Seating arrangements should encourage conversation and interaction, providing comfort while allowing guests to engage with the event and each other.
- Consider the needs of both guests and staff when organizing the layout to ensure smooth operations and efficient service.

Designing the Ideal Trivia Night Schedule:

- The length of a trivia night should strike a balance between providing enough entertainment and avoiding fatigue, typically ranging from one and a half to three hours.
- Understand your audience's preferences and energy levels to determine the optimal time for the event, considering whether they are early birds or night owls.
- Create a schedule that incorporates a variety of rounds, with a mix of exciting and challenging questions, allowing for breaks and building towards an exhilarating climax.

- Incorporate breaks strategically for participants to relax, socialize, and enjoy food and drinks, while also benefiting your revenue.
- A well-structured schedule not only enhances the participants' experience but also helps your team deliver a flawless event by allowing for better planning and coordination.